S0-BYP-741

WITHDRAWN

230
B34g

79508

DATE DUE			
Sep 72			
May 16 73			
Mar 28 74			
Jul 1 75			
Feb 2 7 83			

THE GREAT CONTEST OF
FAITH AND REASON

PIERRE BAYLE

The Great Contest of Faith and Reason

Selections from the Writings of Pierre Bayle

Translated and edited, with an introduction, by
KARL C. SANDBERG
University of Arizona

FREDERICK UNGAR PUBLISHING CO.
NEW YORK

CARL A. RUDISILL LIBRARY
LENOIR RHYNE COLLEGE

230
B34g
79508
Sept. 1972

MILESTONES
OF THOUGHT
in the History of Ideas

General Editors
HANS KOHN
The City College of New York
SIDNEY HOOK
New York University

Copyright © 1963 by
Frederick Ungar Publishing Co., Inc.

Printed in the United States of America

Library of Congress Catalog Card No. 63–12901

INTRODUCTION

TOWARD THE END of his life, Pierre Bayle characterized himself as one who had taken part in the "great contest of faith and reason." No phrase could more accurately describe the generation during which he wrote and thought (1680–1706), for beneath the apparent stability of the French classical age and the apparent order of the reign of Louis XIV, the Enlightenment was preparing, the arms to be used by the Encyclopedists against organized religion were being forged, and two contrary modes of thought were contesting for the minds of the intellectual community of Europe. It was a crucial period in Western thought during which the Age of Faith passed into the Age of Reason.[1]

Faith was belief in the creeds and traditions of Christianity, in a divine Providence which intervened in the affairs of the world, in a God of miracles, and in eternal rewards and punishments. The mind possessed by faith was unafraid of mysteries, the incomprehensible, even on occasion the contradictory, for all objects of belief were founded on the revealed Word of God wherein Christians found the sure answers to the questions of existence. Doctrinal differences between confessions did not change the essential image of faith, for all Christians thought alike on one point —all ultimately referred their queries to a divine authority for final answer. Since the time of St. Augustine faith had ruled as a queen over the intellectual life of Europe. Reason occupied the servants' quarters and had no other role than to defend the dogmas of the faith.

Early in the seventeenth century, however, the hold of faith on the mind of Europe was no longer general. The anarchy and horrors of the wars of religion in sixteenth-cen-

[1] For a comprehensive work on this period see Paul Hazard's *The European Mind: The Critical Years 1680–1715* (New Haven, 1953).

tury France had formed attitudes critical of religion; the discovery of new lands had produced a new awareness of the relativity of peoples and cultures; and Montaigne had opened the Pandora's box of skepticism. Doubt had obscured many of the traditional certainties, and thinking people throughout Europe felt the need of a new oracle which could dispel it.

It was not unexpected that reason, the longtime auxiliary of faith, should be called to grapple with doubt, but the form and scope given to reason by Descartes in his *Discourse on Method* (1637) revealed an entirely new approach to truth. In order to separate the certain from the uncertain, Descartes first rejected all opinions received by tradition and hearsay, and then resolved to accept nothing as true that did not present itself so clearly and evidently that there was no occasion to doubt it. Upon this criterion of truth he developed a rationalism which he felt to be as reliable as the science of mathematics and by means of which he could attain to the knowledge of even the most obscure points if only he avoided drawing unsound conclusions. So contagious was his confidence and so promising was his method that his influence soon spread throughout Europe, and his disciples were found among all groups and confessions.

Few people immediately realized the implication of Descartes' method (least of all Descartes, who used it to prove the existence of God), and for a time the traditional faith and the new rationalism continued to co-exist peaceably. There was nonetheless an irreducible dichotomy between the two. Whereas theology expressed its demands through institutions or creeds and required obedience, reason made the individual the judge of all things. Theology presented the obscurity of mysteries to be accepted. Reason refused to accept anything that was not clear and evident. Theology was encumbered by traditions of doubtful authenticity. Reason became a critical faculty whose mission was to ferret out and label the errors accumulated by the past. Bishop Bossuet was more perspicacious than most of his fellow

defenders of the faith when he said of the Cartesians in
1687: "Under the pretext that one should accept only what
he understands clearly (which is true, within limits) each
one takes the liberty of saying, 'I understand this and I do
not understand that.' On this basis they approve or reject
everything they want, without remembering . . . that in
addition to clear and distinct ideas, we also have general
and vague ideas containing truths so essential that we
would overturn everything if we denied them." The "everything" was to be the general authority and influence of the
Church.

Ironically, the gulf between faith and reason was first
revealed by controversies among the Christian faithful.
Within the Roman Catholic Church, the Jansenists [2] had
been attacking the relaxed morality of the Jesuits [3] since
before 1650. The Jesuits in turn had been trying to convict
the Jansenists of heresy, and both groups were engaged in
a running controversy with the Protestants. All three were
obliged in turn to defend themselves against such heterodox
rationalists as the Socinians.[4] The attempts of each group to
destroy the intellectual foundations of all the others forced
a general reappraisal of the traditional fundaments of belief. Should the decision of the visible Catholic Church be
the authority of last appeal? If so, should the voice of the
councils be heard in preference to that of the Pope, as the
Jansenists maintained, or was the Pope above the councils,
as the Jesuits insisted?

The Protestant writers pointed out that neither party
could prove its allegations and then advanced their own

[2] Disciples of Jansenius (1585–1638), who held severe Augustinian
views of man's freedom, grace, and predestination.

[3] A militant religious order founded by Ignatius of Loyola in
1534 for the conversion of heretics. The first allegiance of the Jesuits
was to the Pope, and they were often accused of being more concerned
with obtaining temporal power and influence than with promoting
spirituality.

[4] Disciples of Faustus Socinus, an Italian theologian (1539–1604),
and forerunners of the modern Unitarians.

claims that the Scripture as interpreted by the individual was to be the rule of faith. But did not the incipient science of textual criticism, which cast doubt upon the authenticity of the Scriptural text, and the increasing divisions within the Protestant movement point to the fallibility of the Protestant principle? Or was reason, which admitted only those ideas which were clear and evident, a more substantial basis for religious belief, even if it precluded acceptance of the deeper mysteries, such as Predestination or the Incarnation? Such was the position of the Arminians [5] of the Reformed Church (Calvinist), the increasing number of Deists, the despised Socinians, and the even more despised Spinoza [6] and his handful of devotees. And if no Christian society could provide a legitimate certainty of its doctrines, would it not be better to remain aloof from all of them? Such questions were being raised with increasing insistency and required answers.

The crisis was hastened by the Catholic persecution of the French Protestants (Huguenots), for with the revocation of the Edict of Nantes in 1685, Protestant liberties in France were suspended, and Catholic missionaries, armed with the secular power of the State, used all kinds of violence to compel the Protestant heretics to return to the true fold. The Huguenot refugees streaming into all countries of Europe raised other questions. Did the possession of truth justify the use of force against heretics? Did the "erring conscience" have any rights? Was not reason a more certain guide here than texts and tradition? A pressing reality compelled people everywhere to confront the questions and form a conclusion.

There was no stopping point in reason's critical examination of Christianity. Theology claimed to have the

[5] Followers of James Arminius, a Dutch theologian (1560–1609), who protested against the tenets of strict Calvinism.

[6] Spinoza (1632–1670) departed radically from the Judeo-Christian tradition by teaching that all reality is One Substance, God, of which thought and tangible matter are but attributes. He also indulged in textual criticism of the Old and New Testaments.

definitive revelation of God's will, but could it give clear and evident answers to the questions concerning Providence, miracles, grace, and evil? Did God intervene in the affairs of the world? How much free will did man possess, if any? If God was all powerful and all good, why was there evil in the world? Here again theology was challenged and found incapable of giving adequate answers. It became more and more evident that the servant reason was deposing faith as the queen and aspiring to reign in her stead.

II

The writings of Pierre Bayle (1647–1706) offer a vivid picture of this generation of intellectual contest, for although Bayle was born in the small and remote town of Carla in Southwestern France, he spent most of his life in the presence of contending doctrines. In fact, his earliest readings were works of religious controversy, for being the son of a Protestant minister who supervised his education, he became aware of the Protestant-Catholic issues from his childhood. In his late adolescence he was also to confront the question of faith and doctrines more directly. When at the age of twenty, he had exhausted the meager educational opportunities available to him in his Protestant milieu, he left with his father's blessing for the Jesuit academy at Toulouse to study logic and philosophy. His sense of fairness caused him to listen to a skillful Catholic polemicist who discussed the question of papal infallibility with him. Young Pierre examined the question, became convinced, and converted to Catholicism. His Jesuit teachers had the chagrin, however, of seeing that their lessons in logic were too effective, for after a year and a half of thought and re-examination, their neophyte decided that he had been converted by specious reasoning, and renouncing his Catholicism, he returned to the Reformed Church (1670).

Reconversion was not without personal risk and sacrifice, for the government of Louis XIV had already begun to use its official influence to discourage heterodoxy and had provided severe penalties against relapsed heretics. Bayle consequently felt it expedient to leave the country. Intending to enter the ministry, he took the road to Geneva where there was a Protestant academy. The new Cartesian philosophy had preceded him there, and he became thoroughly conversant with its principles and spirit. He did not adopt all of them without reservation, but he realized the power of the Cartesian method as a critical tool, especially when coupled with the Scholastic dialectic he had acquired at Toulouse.

At Geneva, his interests broadened, and he felt more attracted to a life of study and erudition than of preaching, but circumstances did not permit him to lead such an untroubled existence. In 1680 after spending six years teaching, first as a private tutor and then as professor of philosophy at the Protestant academy at Sedan, he found himself once more obliged either to abjure his faith or else take the road to exile—the Protestant privileges and liberties in France were rapidly being eroded, and the academy at Sedan had been closed by royal edict. He turned this time to Rotterdam where he had been offered a professorship of philosophy and history in a municipal school.

He took with him a manuscript entitled *Miscellaneous Thoughts on the Comet of 1680*, which he had written as a supposed Catholic, challenging a doctor of the Catholic Sorbonne (a former classmate at Toulouse) on many points. Among Bayle's reflections were the scrutiny of common superstitions about comets, caustic criticism of the moral laxity of Christians (Catholics) in France, and conjectures on the probable morals of a society of atheists. He had not been able to get it published in France, but Holland, free and tolerant, was the great clearing house of ideas, and the work was printed in Rotterdam in 1682.

During the same year Bayle picked up the gauntlet cast down by the Jesuit Father Maimbourg, who had sought to turn public opinion against the Huguenots by writing a derogatory *History of Calvinism.* Bayle's answer to Maimbourg, *A General Critique of "The History of Calvinism,"* won him the reputation of being one of the best Protestant authors, and he continued to answer Catholic objections in his *New Critical Letters* (1684). The increasingly intense persecution of the Protestants still in France also moved him to write a vehement denunciation of Catholic methods, *The True Character of an Entirely Catholic France under the Reign of Louis XIV* (1685). The next year he produced a major work on tolerance entitled *A Philosophic Commentary on These Words of Jesus Christ: "Compel them to come in."* In addition, he undertook to write and publish a monthly literary journal, *The News of the Republic of Letters* (1684–87), consisting of reviews and evaluations of forthcoming books.

Unfortunately, the tensions within the Reformed Church were soon to involve Bayle in conflicts with his fellow Protestants also, for the conservative wing of the Reformed Church in Holland proved to be as intolerant as the Catholics in France. In 1691 Bayle became the object of a vicious attack by the archconservative pastor Pierre Jurieu, who accused him of atheism and sedition. Bayle carried on a lively controversy with Jurieu until 1693 when Jurieu obtained sufficient influence to persuade the city magistrates of Rotterdam to dismiss Bayle from his teaching position. Jurieu's machinations did not drive Bayle from Rotterdam, as he had hoped, but rather permitted the embattled philosopher to devote all of his time to the writing of his *opus magnus,* the four-volume *Historical and Critical Dictionary* (1697). Jurieu had occasion to rue his rashness, for it gave Bayle a distinct antipathy for arrogant theologians, and he carried his controversy with Jurieu and his followers into the *Dictionary.* He had originally intended for the *Dictionary* to be only a compilation of erudition and a correction of historical errors, but he modified it to include many philosophical articles containing not only his own mature thought but also arguments designed to "humble human pride" and silence the contentious. For this purpose he raised endless rational objections to Christian dogmas and insisted more clearly than anyone before had done upon the great gulf between faith and reason.

Because of the philosophic articles, Bayle has often been pictured as a seventeenth-century Voltaire, leading a rational attack on the traditional dogmas of Christianity. It is undeniable that his works were essentially critical and his influence destructive of faith. Voltaire, one of Bayle's great admirers, appears to have evaluated Bayle's influence very accurately in stating that "no one could prove that he was anti-religious, but he turned people away from religion by setting forth the objections to our dogmas so clearly that a lukewarm faith could not but be shaken; and unfortunately most of his readers possess only a lukewarm faith." Bayle was certainly one of the most widely read authors during the eighteenth century, and his *Dictionary* was the arsenal from which the Encyclopedists drew their arms in their struggle against organized religion.

It is improbable, however, that Bayle intended his influence to be so far-reaching. His intent can best be surmised by reading him in his own seventeenth-century context, for he usually wrote only in response to some immediate stimulus. It is also to be noted that the explicit position he assumes in his mature thought is that of a fideist, for whenever he raises rationalistic objections to Christian dogmas, he inevitably insists also on the debility of reason. (There is a remarkable resemblance between the course of his thought and eighteenth-century rationalism which ended with Kant's *Critique of Pure Reason.*) His protests of orthodoxy have traditionally been discounted as insincere gestures of conformity made to get his works approved by the censor, but since there was no censor in Holland and Bayle had no apparent motive to falsify the expression of his thought, it seems best to accept his writings at face value. He is thus much more closely related in spirit to such thinkers as Montaigne, Sir Thomas Browne, and John Dryden than Voltaire and Diderot.

It is significant also that Bayle remained a communicant member of the orthodox Reformed Church until his death and although he wrote against a certain faction of his fellow Protestants, he never severed his religious affiliations. Indeed, after the second edition of the *Dictionary* in 1702, he continued to engage in polemics, but the main body of the Reformed Church was not the object of his critiques. He wrote rather against the rationalistic Arminians to whom he opposed his doctrine of fideism. Voltaire reported that Bayle, at the moment of his death, opened his eyes and exclaimed, "So that is truth!" The story is apocryphal. Actually, Bayle died very quietly in December of 1706 after having corrected the proofs of his latest work on the uses of faith and reason.

III. The Texts

The selections offered here from the *Thoughts on the Comet,* the *Philosophic Commentary,* and the *Dictionary* have been chosen because of the influence which they wielded on subsequent thought. However, in Chapter II shorter passages from his journalistic and polemical writings have been included to give the reader an insight into the nature of the basic conflicts of the time.

In the original, the selections from the *Dictionary* contain some two hundred erudite references which are currently of interest only to the specialist. Only those necessary to the text have been included here.

SELECTED BIBLIOGRAPHY

I. WORKS OF BAYLE

The *Historical and Critical Dictionary,* in English translation. 4 vols. 1734–38. Preceded by Bayle's biography.
Oeuvres diverses, 4 vols. in folio. La Haye, 1737. Contains all
of Bayle's writings except the *Dictionary.*
Selections from Bayle's Dictionary, eds. E. A. Beller and Lee.
Princeton, New Jersey, 1952. 309 pp. Presents repre-
sentative articles from the 1737 translation.

II. WORKS ABOUT BAYLE

Crocker, Lester G. *An Age in Crisis: Man and World in
Eighteenth Century Thought.* Baltimore, 1959. An
analysis of the intellectual issues of the eighteenth century. Shows Bayle's thought, with that of others, in relation to the major currents of the Enlightenment.
Delvolvé, Jean. *Religion critique et philosophie positive chez
Pierre Bayle.* Paris, 1906. A major work on Bayle, pre-
senting an anti-religious interpretation.
Dibon, Paul, ed. *Pierre Bayle, le philosophe de Rotterdam,*
Amsterdam, 1959. A collection of recent studies in English and French on Bayle and his milieu. Shows serious
inadequacies in previous studies and places Bayle among
the believers.
Hazard, Paul. *The European Mind: The Critical Years 1680–
1715.* Trans. Lewis May. New Haven, 1953. Contains a
penetrating analysis of Bayle's times in addition to a
very good chapter on Bayle's work and influence.
Robinson, Howard. *Bayle the Skeptic.* New York, 1931. A
rationalistic view of Bayle. Contains a relatively complete bibliography.

CONTENTS

CONTENTS

Chapter I

REASON, SUPERSTITION,
AND TRADITION

[Among the superstitions accumulated by the ages
was the belief that comets were presages of misfortunes, signs of divine wrath, or instruments of baleful
influences upon the world and its inhabitants. When
a brilliant comet appeared in 1680, the question of the
portent and influence of comets was again raised.
Bayle undertook to examine the question critically and
rationally. The result was his *Miscellaneous Thoughts
on the Comet of 1680* of which selections are presented here. This work was a loosely-constructed as-
semblage of disparate ideas which Bayle had originally intended for a former fellow student who was
now a doctor of the Sorbonne and a prominent member of the dominant Catholic Church. In it is seen one
of the first great manifestations of the new rationalism,
probing, questioning, and challenging the commonly
held beliefs and authorities of the past. The Christian
faith was to suffer from this examination because the
same reasons given to support the superstitions concerning comets had often been used to defend the
dogmas of religion.]

MISCELLANEOUS THOUGHTS ON THE COMET OF 1680 WRITTEN
TO A DOCTOR OF THE SORBONNE WHEREIN IT IS PROVED BY
SEVERAL REASONS DRAWN FROM PHILOSOPHY AND THEOLOGY
THAT COMETS ARE NOT PRESAGES OF MISFORTUNES

III. *There is no valid reason for believing that comets are omens.*

Everyday I hear people reasoning upon the nature of comets, and although I am an astronomer neither in name nor in fact, I study carefully everything written on the subject by those who are the most capable. Still I must confess to you that I am convinced by none of their arguments except those against the popular error that comets threaten the world with a host of desolations.

I am therefore all the more at a loss to understand how such a learned person as you could be swept along with the flood with everyone else, imagining that comets appear as heralds sent to proclaim that God has declared war on the human race. You should be convinced, on the contrary, even if for no more reason than having successfully predicted the return of the comet, that comets are not signs or wonders which follow no fixed rule, but rather bodies subject to the ordinary laws of nature. If you were a preacher I would forgive you for your persuasion, for these fearful thoughts lend themselves naturally to the most elaborate and moving adornments of eloquence. Moreover, they acquire more esteem for the one who voices them and make a much greater impression upon the minds of his listeners than do a hundred other propositions which are proved demonstrably. But when I see a scholar who has nothing to gain by convincing people of anything and who ought to nourish his mind only upon pure reason, I cannot approve of his holding such poorly substantiated opinions and being satisfied with the reasons offered by tradition, poets, and historians.

IV. *Concerning the credibility of poets*

It is not possible to have a sorrier foundation for one's argument. You are not unaware, sir, that they are so intent upon strewing pompous descriptions throughout their works, such as tales of wonders and marvelous adventures of their heroes, that to accomplish their purposes they imagine a thousand astonishing incidents. Thus, far from believing upon their word that the overthrow of the Roman Republic was caused by two or three comets, I would not even believe that comets appeared at that time unless someone else so testified. After all, we must admit that a man who has taken it into his head to write a poem has gained control, as it were, over all the workings of nature. The heavens and the earth do not move except by his command; eclipses or shipwrecks appear if he sees fit; all of the elements are moved about according to his convenience. We see armies in the air and monsters on the earth in as great a number as he wishes; the angels and the devils make their appearance every time that he so ordains; even the gods, mounted on machines, hold themselves in readiness to satisfy his needs, and as he has a special need of comets because of the popular misconception concerning them, he seizes upon readymade comets which he finds in histories; and if he does not find them there, he manufactures them himself and lends to them the color and aspect most likely to show that heaven has taken a very distinguished interest in the business at hand. After that, who would not laugh at the spectacle of a throng of intelligent people trying to prove the malignity of these new comets by nothing more than the writings of Virgil, Claudius, and other poets of antiquity.

V. *Concerning the authority of historians*

As for the historians, I admit they do not take the liberty of inventing extraordinary happenings as the poets do.

Nevertheless, in most of them we see such a keen desire to
report all of the miracles and visions sanctioned by the
credulity of the common people that it would not be pru-
dent to believe everything they recount about the supernatural. I do not know whether they think their histories
would appear too simple if they did not mingle a great number of wonders and supernatural accidents with the things
which happen in the normal course of the world. Or perhaps they hope that this kind of seasoning, which is much
to the natural taste of people, will maintain the interest of
their reader by constantly giving him occasion to marvel.
Or perhaps they believe that their history will be more distinguished in the future if they include the account of these
wondrous doings. But however that may be, no one can
deny that historians take a great pleasure in compiling
everything that smacks of the miraculous. Livy gives us a
solid proof of this, because in spite of his great intelligence
and the nearly perfect history that he left us, he nonetheless fell into the error of leaving us an unbearable collection
of all of the ridiculous wonders which, according to pagan
superstition, required men to offer oblations to the gods.
(This is the reason, say some, for which Pope Gregory
condemned his works to be burned.) And what a disorder
we find in all of the immense volumes which contain the
records of various orders of our monks! It seems that they
took jealous pleasure in indiscriminately amassing all sorts
of imaginary miracles for no other purpose than outdoing
their rival orders. I say this just between ourselves, because
you know that in order not to irritate these good fathers
and to avoid scandalizing the common people, we must not
publicize the defects of their records. We will simply be
satisfied not to read them ourselves.

We see all around us examples of a close relationship
between poetry and history. Many people assure us upon
the authority of Cicero and Quintilian "that history is
poetry freed from the restrictions of versification" and cite
the testimony of Lucian "that the ship of history will be
heavy and motionless if the breeze of poetry does not fill

its sails." They tell us that one has to be a poet in order to be a historian, the difference between poetry and history being almost imperceptible. I am surprised that those who have taught us so many fine things have not seen that they were furnishing a good pretext to the critics who might maintain that historians are indeed very much like poets in that they both fill their works with wonders and fictions. How fortunate are those two excellent poets who are now working on the history of *Louis the Great,* which is full of real wonders, because without indulging in fiction they can satisfy the overruling desire which possesses poets and historians to recount everything extraordinary.

In spite of all of that, sir, I am not one to quarrel over the authority of historians. In spite of their credulity, I will agree that comets appeared as often as they report and that in the years which followed the apparition of comets there were just as many misfortunes as they contend. I acquiesce to all of that. But this is all that I will grant you and all that you should reasonably claim. You see what I am driving at. I defy you to conclude, in spite of all of your subtlety, that the comets were either the sign or the cause of the misfortunes which followed their apparition. Thus, the testimony of historians proves nothing more than the fact that comets appeared and that afterwards there were indeed disorders or misfortunes in the world. Now this is very far from proving that one of these two things was either the cause or the sign of the other. What would you think of a woman on Saint Honoré Street who saw carriages passing every time she put her head out of the window and concluded that she caused the carriages to pass, or at least that she was an omen to all of the neighborhood that every time she came to the window, carriages would soon pass by?

VII. *Concerning the authority of tradition*

After what I have just said, a detailed refutation of the unreasonable deference given to tradition would be superfluous. It is obvious that if there is some legitimate foundation for the opinion which people have had about comets from time immemorial, it consists entirely of the testimony which histories and other books have given. Therefore, if this testimony is of no value, as I have shown and as it will appear even more clearly by what I have yet to say, we should no longer give any consideration to the number of opinions founded on it.

If we could only see what goes on in the minds of men when they choose an opinion! I am sure we would find the basis of an opinion now held by multitudes to be nothing more than the authority of two or three persons who supposedly had thoroughly examined the doctrine they set forth. Their apparent competence caused a few people to believe their teaching, and these in turn persuaded others who felt it more convenient to accept the new teaching uncritically than to examine it carefully. The ever-increasing number of credulous and slothful disciples thus became a new reason for still other men to forego the difficulty of examining an opinion which they saw to be so widespread, for they believed naively that this doctrine had become popular only because of the soundness of the reasons which had originally established it. Finally, men saw themselves reduced to the necessity of believing what everyone else believed for fear of appearing to be quarrelsome dissidents who, presuming to know more than all other peoples, contradicted a venerable antiquity. It was therefore counted a merit to examine nothing and to rely wholly on tradition. Judge for yourself if the suffrage of even 100,000,000 men can make an opinion probable if they have received it in this way. Tell me, then, if I am not right in saying that the basis of a popular belief which is supposedly founded upon the testimony of a multitude of disciples is really nothing more than the authority of two or three people who apparently examined what they were teaching. You will remember, sir, that certain fictitious opinions have recently been discredited in spite of the great number of witnesses in their favor, because it was shown that these witnesses had simply copied each other uncritically, and together made only one witness instead of a multitude. In view of these facts, you must conclude that even though several nations throughout several centuries have all blamed comets for all the disasters which followed their apparition, their opinion is not more probable than if seven or eight people advanced it, because there are scarcely more than that who have believed it after examining it according to the principles of philosophy.

VIII. *Reasons for not commenting on the authority of philosophers*

Should I tell you why I have not examined the authority of the philosophers in the same way as I have that of the poets and the historians? It is because I am persuaded that the philosophers have had no effect upon your mind except to make popular tradition more general. I do not believe you accept the reasons upon which they base their testimony, for you are too clever to be the dupe of any philosopher, provided that he attacks you only by the way of reasoning. (I must grant you that in things which you believe to be in the domain of reason you follow only pure reason.) It is therefore not the philosophers as such who have contributed to your credulity on this occasion, since it is certain that all of their reasonings in favor of malevolent influences are pitiful. Should I tell you as one old friend to another why it is that you have fallen into a common opinion without consulting the oracle of reason? It is because you believe there is something divine in all of this, as people who came after the famous Hippocrates used to say of certain sicknesses. It is because you imagine that the general consent of so many nations in so many consecutive centuries can only come from a kind of inspiration, *vox populi, vox Dei,* the voice of the people is the voice of God. It is because you are accustomed by your theological mind to abandon reason as soon as you believe yourself to be in the presence of a mystery. This docility is very laudable, but when one gives it too free a rein, it trespasses on the rights of reason, as Mr. Pascal has very well pointed out. Finally, it is because your fearful mind very easily leads you to believe that the corruption of the world puts the most dreadful plagues in the hand of God, which the good Lord nonetheless does not wish to hurl upon the earth without having seen whether men will repent, as He did before sending the Flood. All of that, my good sir, creates an illusion of authority in your mind, against which all of your dialectic skill is of little avail.

While you are in this frame of mind, I must not think that I could free you from your errors by reasoning with you upon the principles of philosophy. I must either leave you where you are or else reason upon principles of piety and religion. I will do the latter (for I do not want you to escape me), after having set down for your consideration several reasons founded upon common sense which demonstrate the temerity of that opinion which people hold concerning the influence of comets. . . .

[Bayle found many arguments with which to refute the common belief in presages: comets do not have the power to cause anything to happen on earth; even if they did, their effects could just as well be good as bad; astrology, which is the foundation of the belief in the supernatural import of comets, is nothing but a ridiculous superstition; in the years immediately following the apparition of comets there have been no more misfortunes than at other times; if comets were really omens of misfortune, God would have performed miracles in order to confirm the pagans in their idolatry, since the superstitious pagans could only have redoubled their devotion to their gods, which were the only ones they knew; and finally the belief that comets were omens is only a pagan superstition introduced and maintained in Christianity by the excessive deference for tradition and antiquity.

But Bayle's thoughts on the comet were not the most important part of his book. Wishing to refute every possible objection to his theological reasons he undertook in a long digression to prove that God did not make comets appear among the pagans in order to make known his providence and to keep them from falling into atheism. God, he argued, does not dispel one error by establishing another; comets are not capable of preventing atheism; atheism is not a greater evil than idolatry; neither the mind nor the heart of the idolater is preferable to that of the atheist; and atheism does not necessarily lead to immorality. Bayle thus subjected to rational scrutiny the commonplace that religious belief and moral conduct were inseparable. In making conduct depend principally on temperament (an idea closely related to the Calvinist view of human nature) and in showing that a society of atheists would not differ from the Catholic Christian society of seventeenth-century France, Bayle hastened the dissolution of the moral authority of religion in the minds of his readers.]

XXXIII. *Atheism does not necessarily lead to corruption of morals.*

People are persuaded only by a false preconception concerning the light of conscience that atheism is the most abominable state into which anyone may fall, for not having discerned our true motives, they imagine that our beliefs determine our acts. This is the way they reason. Man is naturally reasonable, he never desires without a conscious motive, he necessarily seeks happiness and flees unhappiness, and he gives his preference to the objects most agreeable to him. Therefore, if he is convinced that there is a Providence which governs the world, from whose workings nothing escapes, which rewards the virtuous with an infinite bliss and punishes the wicked with an eternal torment, he will infallibly follow after virtue and flee vice. He will renounce all carnal pleasures, knowing on the one hand that these fleeting moments of gratification will procure him an eternity of pain, and feeling on the other hand that in depriving himself of them he will find an eternity of bliss. But if he does not believe in Providence, he will regard his desires as his ultimate end and the rule of all his acts. He will scoff at what others call virtue and integrity and will follow only the movements of his own lusts. If possible, he will do away with all those who displease him. He will perjure himself for the slightest gain, and if his position puts him above human laws, as he has already placed himself above the remorse of conscience, there is no crime which we should not expect of him. He is a monster infinitely more dangerous than those fierce beasts, those lions and mad bulls from which Hercules delivered Greece. Someone else, who had nothing to fear from men, could at least be restrained by the fear of the gods, which has always been a means of bridling the passions of men. And it is sure that many crimes were prevented among the pagans by the care taken to preserve the memory of all the striking punishments visited upon scoundrels for their supposed impiety, or even to invent a few examples, such as the story spread abroad in the time of Augustus when a temple in Asia had been pillaged by the soldiers of Mark Anthony. It was said that the one who first laid his hand upon the altar of the goddess who was worshipped in that temple had immediately been struck blind and had become paralyzed in all the members of his body. (Wanting to verify the report, Augustus learned from the old officer who had done the deed that he had not only been sound and healthy ever since, but also that this act had put him in comfortable circumstances for the rest of his life). . . . People reason that all of these accounts, true or false, which had such a good effect upon the mind of an idolater, have no power over an atheist. He is so impervious to all of these considerations that he must necessarily be the most accomplished and incorrigible scoundrel in the world.

CXXXIV. *Experience opposes the idea that*
the knowledge of God checks the evil
inclinations of men.

All of that is well and good when we regard that the-
oretical side of the question and make metaphysical abstrac-
tions of it, but unfortunately, the theory does not square
with the findings of experience. Suppose that we asked inhabitants of another world to predict the morals of Christians after telling them that Christians are creatures endowed with reason and good sense, avid of happiness, and
persuaded that there is a Paradise for those who obey the
law of God and a Hell for those who do not. I admit they
would undoubtedly assure us that the Christians strive to
excel in observing the precepts of the Gospel and vie to
distinguish themselves in works of mercy, in prayer, and
in forgiving offenses, if there be any among them capable of
offending his neighbor. But why would they make this com-
plimentary judgment? It is because they would have considered only an abstract idea of the Christians, for if they
considered them individually and saw everything that
makes them act, they would soon lower the good opinion
that they would have formed, and they would not have
lived two weeks among us without declaring that in this
world people do not conduct themselves according to the
light of conscience.

CXXXV. *The reason for the disparity*
between belief and practice

Here we come to the real solution of this question.
When we compare the real morals of a man who has a religion
with the abstract idea of what his morals should be, we are
surprised not to find any conformity between reality and
our expectations. According to our abstract idea, we should
expect that a man who believes in a God, a Paradise, and a

Hell would do everything that he knew to be pleasing to God and would do nothing he knew to be displeasing to Him, but the life of this man shows us that he does just the opposite. Do you wish to know the cause of this incongruity? Here it is—man does not decide between two possible actions by his abstract knowledge of duty, but by the particular judgment he makes of each one as he is on the point of acting. Now this decision may well be in conformity with his abstract idea of duty, but most often it is not. It is almost always determined by the dominant passion of the heart, the inclination of the temperament, the force of habit, and the taste and sensitivity which one has for certain things. The poet who has Medea say, "I see and approve the good, but I do evil" [1] has depicted perfectly the difference between the light of conscience and the particular judgment which moves us to act. Conscience recognizes the beauty of virtue in the abstract and forces us to agree that nothing is more praiseworthy than to live virtuously. But when the heart is once possessed by an unlawful love, when one sees that he will experience pleasure in satisfying it and will be plunged into chagrin and unbearable anxiety if he does not satisfy it, no light of conscience is of any avail. Nothing is consulted except passion, and judgment is rendered in favor of acting here and now against the abstract idea of duty. All of these observations only go to show that nothing is more illusory than to judge the moral character of a man by the general opinions with which he is imbued. . . .

CXXXVI. *Man does not act according to his principles.*

Say what you will about man being a reasonable creature. It is nonetheless true that his conduct is almost never consistent with his principles. In speculative questions he is

[1] Ovid, *Metamorphosis*, book 7.

quite capable of avoiding fallacious conclusions, because in these matters he sins much more by accepting false premises than by drawing false conclusions from them, but it is quite another thing in questions of morals. Here he very seldom adopts false principles and almost never abandons the ideas of natural equity in his conscience, and yet he almost always concludes in favor of his dissolute desires. Why is it, pray tell me, that in spite of the prodigious diversity of opinions concerning the way of serving God and living honorably, we see certain passions reigning constantly in all countries and in all ages? Why is it that ambition, avarice, envy, the desire for vengeance, fornication, and all the crimes that can satisfy these passions are seen everywhere? Why is it that the Jew and the Mohammedan, the Turk and the Moor, the Christian and the pagan, the Indian and the Tartar, the islander and the mainlander, the noble and the commoner, all of these kinds of people who in all other things are alike only in their abstract humanity, why is it that they are so alike with respect to these passions that they seem only to copy one another? Where can we find the reason for all of this except in the idea that the true principle of man's actions (I except those in whom the Holy Spirit operates with all of its efficacity) is nothing else than the temperament, the natural inclination for pleasure, the taste contracted for certain objects, the desire to please, a habit contracted through association with one's friends, or some other disposition which results from the essence of our nature, no matter where we were born or what we have been taught?

My explanation must be sound since the ancient pagans, who had an unbelievable baggage of superstitions, who were constantly appeasing the wrath of their gods, who were frightened by an endless number of wonders because they believed the gods to be the dispensers of prosperity and adversity according to one's conduct, still did not fail to commit every crime imaginable. And if my explanation were not true, how would it be possible for the Christians, who know so clearly by a revelation supported by so many miracles that they must renounce vice to be eternally happy and to avoid eternal misery; who have so many excellent preachers who are paid to compose and deliver the most cogent and compelling exhortations to virtue; who everywhere have so many learned and zealous spiritual advisers; how then would it be possible, I say, for the Christians to live as they do in the most terrible licentiousness and vice?

CXLV. *The pagans, who believed firmly in many gods, were not more virtuous than atheists would be.*

No matter how often you object that the fear of a God is an eminently suitable means of correcting the natural corruption of man, I will still invoke the testimony of experience and ask why the pagans, who carried the fear of their gods to excessive superstitions, were so lax in correcting this corruption that every abominable vice reigned among them. In spite of the ever present memory of spectacular retribution visited by the heavens upon blasphemers and perjurers and those guilty of sacrilege; in spite of the tales forged to make the wicked tremble; in spite of the pompous descriptions of the Furies, Hell, and the Elysian Fields, temples were still pillaged when the occasion was propitious and false witnesses were found in great profusion. Juvenal is inimitable in his picture of false witnesses who have no religion and false witnesses who believe in a God. He says that the former perjure themselves without hesitation, whereas the latter reason for some time and then perjure themselves with extreme confidence. They subsequently feel remorse and imagine that the vengeance of God pursues them everywhere. Nonetheless they do not mend their ways, but sin as readily at the next opportunity as they did before.

The picture is an exact copy of Nature. We still see this same spirit reigning everywhere and drawing men to sin in spite of the fear of Hell and the remorse of conscience. So true is this observation that to argue against my thesis is nothing else than pitting metaphysical reasonings against a fact, in the manner of that philosopher [Zeno] who attempted to prove that there was no movement. No one, I am sure, will object to my use of the method of Diogenes who without answering the subtleties of Zeno point by point merely walked in his presence. Indeed, nothing is more efficacious in showing an honest man that he is reasoning upon false hypotheses than to show him that he is arguing against experience. . . .

As I have already said, we have no annals informing us of the morals and customs of a nation completely immersed in atheism. We cannot therefore refute by established fact that atheists are incapable of any moral virtue and that they are ferocious beasts more to be feared than lions and tigers. But it is not difficult to show that this conjecture is highly uncertain. For since experience shows us that those who believe in a Paradise and a Hell are capable of committing all sorts of crimes, it is evident that the inclination to do evil does not come from the ignorance of God's existence and that it is not corrected by acquiring the knowledge of a God who punishes and rewards. One may conclude therefrom that the inclination to do evil is not any greater in a soul destitute of the knowledge of God than in a soul which knows God.

CLXI. *Conjectures upon the morals of a society of atheists*

Now after all these remarks, if you wish to know my conjectures concerning a society of atheists, I will not hesitate to say that with regard to morals and civic affairs, it would be just like a society of pagans. It is true that very strict and well-executed laws would be needed for the punishing of criminals, but are they not needed everywhere? Would we dare to leave our houses if theft, murder, and other violences were permitted by the laws of the sovereign? In the streets of Paris, both day and night, are we protected from thieves and pickpockets by anything more than the strict enforcement of the king's laws? Without his laws, would we not be exposed to the same violences as in former reigns, even though our teachers and confessors discharged their duties even better than they formerly did? In spite of the rack, the zeal of the magistrate, and the diligence of the provost, how many murders and thefts are committed even in the places of public execution and at the moment when criminals are being executed? We can say without indulging in false oratory that human justice is the cause of the virtue of most people, for as soon as it fails to punish the sinner, few people keep themselves from the sin.

CLXXII. *In a society of atheists there would be laws of propriety and honor.*

We can now see how apparent it is that a society of atheists would practice both civic and moral actions just as other societies practice them, provided that crimes were severely punished and that honor and shame were associated with certain acts. Ignorance of a Supreme Being, the Creator and Preserver of the world, would not make the members of this society impervious to glory and scorn, to reward and punishment, and to all the passions which are seen in other men, nor would it extinguish in them the light of reason. In a society of atheists we should therefore expect to see people who would be honest in their business dealings, who would help the poor, who would oppose injustice, who would be faithful to their friends, who would scorn insults addressed to them, who would restrain their carnal appetites and who would do harm to no one. Their motives, it is true, would vary, for some would desire to be praised for all these splendid actions which the public would surely approve, while others would do them with the intention of acquiring the support of friends and protectors in case of need. Women would pride themselves on their chastity, because this quality infallibly procures them the love and esteem of men. I do not doubt that there would be crimes committed of every kind, but no more than are committed in societies of idolaters, because everything which motivates pagans, whether to good or evil, would be found in a society of atheists, that is, rewards and punishments, glory and shame, temperament and education. For as concerning this sanctifying grace which fills us with the love of God and which gives us victory over our evil habits, the pagans are just as bereft of it as atheists.

Do you wish to be fully convinced that a people deprived of the knowledge of God would make rules of honor for themselves and observe them scrupulously? You have only to look among the Christians to see a certain worldly honor which is directly contrary to the spirit of the Gospel. I would be curious to know the origin of this system of honor of which the Christians are so idolatrous and to which they sacrifice everything. When they believe that it is dishonorable to leave an offense unpunished, or to yield the first place to another, or to have less ambition or pride than their equals, is it because they believe in a God, a Gospel, a resurrection, a Paradise, and a Hell? You will surely grant me the point. Examine all of the ideas of propriety which are found among the Christians, and you will scarcely find two which have been borrowed from religion. Moreover, when improper actions become proper, it is not at all because people have consulted the morality of the Gospel. Some time ago women took it into their heads that it was more fashionable to dress in public and in presence of other people than in private, to ride horseback, to give frenetic chase to some wild animal during the hunt, etc., and because these actions have become common, we no longer look upon them as immodest. Was it religion which changed our ideas in this respect? Compare the manners of several nations which profess Christianity. Compare them, I say, one with another, and you will see that what is accounted improper in one country is not at all improper elsewhere. It must then be that the ideas of propriety which are among the Christians do not come from the religion that they profess. I admit that some of their ideas are universal, for we have no example of a Christian nation where it is shameful for women to be chaste. But to act in good faith we must confess that this idea is older than both the Gospel and Moses. It is a certain impression which is as old as the world. . . . Let us admit, then, that there are ideas of honor in the human race implanted there by nature, that is, by a general Providence. Let us especially admit that such is the case of that honor of which the brave among us are so jealous and which is so in opposition to the law of God. And how can we doubt after that, that nature could do among the atheists, where the knowledge of the Gospel would not oppose it, that which it does among the Christians?

CLXXIII. *Belief in the mortality of the soul does not prevent people from desiring to immortalize their name.*

Perhaps people imagine that the desire to immortalize one's name, which has so much power over the minds of other men, has no effect on an atheist, who is persuaded that his soul dies with his body. But this thought is quite false, because it is certain that those who have done great deeds in order to be praised by posterity were not flattered by the hope of knowing in the next world what people would say about them after their death. We find examples even today in our brave men of war who expose themselves to so many perils and hardships in order to have their name mentioned in history. Do they imagine that the monuments which will be erected in their honor and which will inform their most distant posterity of everything great and magnificent which they have done, do they imagine, I say, that these monuments will cause them to feel any pleasure? Do they believe that they will be informed in the next world of what is happening in this one? And whether they enjoy the bliss of Paradise or whether they burn in Hell, do they not know that it would be quite useless to learn that men admire them? Therefore, it is not the belief in the immortality of the soul which causes people to love glory, and consequently atheists are quite capable of desiring an eternal reputation. The most substantial part of the love of glory is a pleasant image which one caresses in his mind during this life of many successive centuries filled with admiration for one's deeds. And after one is dead? This thought is of no further use, for there are many other things to do besides thinking of the reputation which one has left in this world.

You have no doubt heard that when M. de Castelnau was awarded the baton of a marshal of France just before his death, he said all that was very fine in this world, but he was going to depart for a country where it would be of no use to him.

CLXXIV. *Examples which show that atheists have not been especially conspicuous by the impurity of their morals*

I will perhaps be told that it would nonetheless be a strange thing for an atheist to live virtuously, a veritable prodigy beyond the forces of nature. I answer that it is not any stranger for an atheist to live virtuously than it is for a Christian to commit all sorts of crimes. If we see the latter prodigy every day, why should we believe that the other is impossible? But I will give you some even stronger reasons to show you that what I have set forth concerning the morals of a society of atheists is more than mere conjecture. I will point out that those few persons among the ancients who made an open profession of atheism, such as Diagoras,

Theodorus, Evmerus and several others, caused no general outcry by their libertinism. Although they have been accused of dreadful aberrations in their reason, I am not aware that they have the reputation of extraordinary licentiousness in their conduct. On the contrary, I find that their conduct appeared so admirable to Clement of Alexandria that he felt obliged to protest against the accusation of atheism that was leveled at them. He maintained that their reputation for impiety was due only to their great zeal and perspicacity in pointing out the errors of pagan theology, and that they were called atheists only because they refused to recognize the false pagan gods. . . .

Epicurus, who denied Providence and the immortality of the soul, was one of the philosophers of antiquity who lived in the most exemplary way, and although his sect was subsequently brought into disrepute, it is nonetheless certain that it was composed of many honorable and upright persons, and those who dishonored it by their vices were not corrupted by this school. They were people who gave themselves over to debauchery by habit and temperament and who were glad to cover their filthy passions with such a good pretext as that of following the maxims of one of the greatest philosophers in the world. They were the kind of people who imagined that as long as they hid themselves under the mantle of philosophy they could scoff at the scandal they caused. They did not become inclined to vice because they had embraced the doctrine of Epicurus, but they embraced the doctrine of Epicurus, which they did not understand, because they were inclined to vice. At least this is what Seneca says, and although he belonged to a sect which detested the memory of Epicurus, he does not hesitate to voice his belief that the pleasures of this philosopher were very sober and restrained. St. Jerome speaks very advantageously of the frugality of the same Epicurus and holds him up in sharp contrast to the licentiousness of the Christians, in order to shame the latter.

Among the Jews there was a sect which frankly denied

the immortality of the soul. I speak of the Sadducees. I am not aware that with such a detestable opinion they led a life any more corrupt than the other Jews, and on the contrary it is very likely that they were more upright than the Pharisees, who prided themselves so much on their observation of the law of God.

Mr. de Balzac informs us in *The Christian Socrates* of the last words of a prince who had lived and died an atheist and he testifies that he lacked no moral virtues, swore only by "certainly," drank only herb tea, and was extremely circumspect in every outward appearance.

The detestable Vanini, who was burned in Toulouse for his atheism in 1619, had always lived moderately, and whoever would have accused him of any criminal deviation, except in his dogmas, would have run a great risk of being convicted of slander.

Under the reign of Charles IX in 1573, a man who had secretly affirmed his atheism was burned in Paris. He maintained that there was no other god in the world except the purity of his body. He was therefore reported to be yet a virgin. He had as many shirts as there are days of the year, and he sent them to Flanders to be washed in a fountain famed for the purity of its water and its property of making clothes admirably white. He had an aversion for all kinds of impurities, whether in acts or in words, and although he upheld his blasphemies with a stubbornness which he retained until his death, he always stated them in an extremely mild way.

You cannot be unaware of the account given by Mr. Ricaut, Secretary of the Count of Winchelsey, the English ambassador at Constantinople. I need not comment upon the diligence and exactitude of this author. I will say only that after giving the account of a numerous sect of atheists formed in Turkey, composed mostly of cadis and of people versed in Arabic literature, he adds that the partisans of this sect have an extraordinary affection for one another, that they render each other all kinds of good services, that they are civil and hospitable, and that if a guest of their persuasion arrives they provide him with the best food they have. I do not deny that their civilities go too far, since they provide their guest with a most improper recreation during the night, but in that they do nothing of which the other Turks are not guilty. Therefore, if we compare the life of the other Turks with that of these atheists, we will find either that there is no difference between the two or that the former are less virtuous than the latter.

I will certainly not put the Chancellor de l'Hospital among the number of atheists, for I have no doubt but that he was a good Christian. I will simply state that he was very strongly suspected of having no religion, although he lived in a most exemplary way and no one appeared to be more austere, more sober, or more dignified than he was. Mr. de Beaucaire de Peguillon, Bishop of Metz, frankly accuses him of atheism. His testimony is a little suspect because of his attachment to the Cardinal of Lorraine, whose tutor he had been. But this example nonetheless shows us that men are very careless when they state so boldly that atheism is inseparable from vice, since a Chancellor of France was suspected of atheism, although his good life was known by everybody. . . .

[After this digression on atheism Bayle returns to the comet and finishes the book with various observations on political and moral themes.]

Chapter II

REASON AND THE
WAYS OF BELIEF

[The fundamental question of the religious controversy of 1680–1685 centered around the rule of faith,
and throughout Europe people were asking (or answering) the question, "Why is one party more believable than another?" As a Protestant writer, Bayle
walked an intellectual tightrope, for he had to confront the challenges offered by the claim to papal infallibility on the Catholic side and the Socinian and
Deistic insistence on a thoroughly rational religion on
the other. Early in his life Bayle had found the strong
and the weak side of the Catholic claim. In the following selection, while answering Father Maimbourg's
History of Calvinism, Bayle gives his reasons for rejecting the way of authority.]

GENERAL CRITIQUE OF "THE HISTORY OF CALVINISM"

*The privilege of infallibility cannot be
gratuitously assumed.*

Putting all ceremonies aside, I will first of all ask these
infallible gentlemen how they know that they are infallible.
They should not find it strange for me to ask this question,
because they have no justification for asking us to believe
them simply upon their word, especially when it is a question of the greatest and most extraordinary manifestations
of the mercy of God. They should remember that if they
are mistaken on this point, they are risking not only their
own salvation but also that of all Christians. If they are

falsely persuaded that they are infallible, they will readily believe everything that comes to their mind. Moreover, the people who believe them infallible, will receive all of their extravagances without any scruple, for not daring to trust their own reason when it differs with the church which they hold to be infallible, they will not be able to recognize the falsity of anything. Therefore, when a church claims the privilege of infallibility, it is of the greatest importance that it demonstrate by clear and incontestable reasons that it possesses this great and rare treasure.

The doctrine of infallibility must be established by unequivocal declarations of the Scripture.

I will ask them in the second place if this admirable privilege is a pure gift of the Holy Spirit. This they cannot deny. Therefore, it is not possible for them to claim infallibility except by virtue of revelation. Thus, the Roman Church is obliged to show us by the Scripture that God has established among men an infallible tribunal, which was to be the Communion of Rome. The passages of the Scripture which contain these truths must be so clear that no one could be mistaken in their interpretation, so clear, in fact, that each of the faithful can recognize by the light of his own mind that God indeed declares these truths in these passages. But now suppose that these passages were susceptible of several reasonable interpretations and that without doing the least violence to the Scripture and without contradicting any other principle of the faith, one could refrain from giving them the meaning of the infallibility of the Church. Would it not be obvious that each person would be free to believe about it what he wished? In this case, the dogma of the infallibility of the Church would no longer be binding upon the conscience. These passages, therefore, must witness so clearly in favor of the infallibility of the Church that they do not admit of any contrary interpretation.

I insist on this point because if a passage which supposedly declares the infallibility of the Roman Church is given several diverse interpretations, the all-powerful authority of the Church cannot be invoked to render the "true" meaning until this infallibility has already been established. We are trying to find out if an infallible authority is to be had among the Christians. We examine the right claimed by the Roman Church. During the investigation this right must remain inoperative. It would be absurd to interpose the authority of the Roman Church to give the passage the meaning necessary to establish the very infallibility which is in question. Therefore, since we do not yet know if the Scripture has established an infallible judge among the Christians, it follows that we cannot yet be obliged to defer to any interpretation emanating from this judge. Consequently, it is necessary that we be able to discover without the help of the Church that the Holy Spirit has indeed revealed the infallibility of the Church in these passages. . . .

Having posed these conditions I will say in the third place that it is impossible for the Roman Church ever to prove that it is infallible, for in order to do so (as I have just established), it must produce passages from the Scripture which contain this infallibility so clearly that the common people can there recognize it without the intervention of the Church. Now there are no passages of this nature in the Holy Scripture, as I shall demonstrate. Therefore it is impossible for the Roman Church ever to prove that it is infallible.

*The very manner in which the Roman
Church attempts to prove its infallibility
establishes the validity of the Protestant
principle of individual examination.*

In order to prove that there are no passages in the Scripture in which the common people can recognize the infallibility of the Church without the intervention of the

Church, I will first advance a reason which opposes the infallibility of the Church by infallibility itself. Indeed, if the people can recognize the infallibility of the Church in the Scripture without the intervention of the Church, it follows that with regard to certain passages, at least, the Scripture is the only judge of controversy. The people do not need any infallible authority in order to understand the revelation and to possess one of the principal articles of their faith. It is certain, moreover, that the passages which contain the promise of the infallibility of the Church (supposing that they do) are the most difficult to interpret in all the Scripture. It therefore follows that if the people can understand them without the aid of an infallible authority, they can also understand the rest of the Scripture without the help of the Church. Consequently, we have no need of an infallible tribunal. If we can get along without it for the most obscure points of doctrine, we can get along without it for the others. You see that the infallibility of the Roman Church is almost like those propositions which the logicians call *seipsas falsificiantes*, for the very means (examination of the Scripture) which the Church uses to establish its infallibility shows that its infallibility is not necessary. . . .

Divisions within the Roman Church refute its claim to infallibility.

But here in my opinion is the strongest reason that can be advanced to prove that the passages of Scripture which speak of the infallibility of the Church are not sufficiently clear for the people to understand them: these passages are so obscure that the Church itself does not understand them. It is easy to be assured of this point by considering that there are two great parties in the Communion of Rome which differ greatly with one another concerning the seat of infallibility within the Church. One of them maintains that the Pope alone received this privilege from Jesus Christ. The other party claims that the Universal Church

represented by the general Councils received it. Each of
these two parties is obliged to go to the Scripture in order
to justify its claims and produce its original deeds and
patents of nobility. But what happens? The partisans of the
Pope maintain that the interpretation of passages alleging
the infallibility of the Councils is false. The other party
makes the same charge, for the partisans of the Councils
maintain that the interpretation of the passages alleging
the infallibility of the Pope is contrary to the written and
unwritten word of God. At this point, it becomes clear to
any man of common sense that the passages of Scripture
which concern infallibility are not easy to understand. If
they were, they would speak clearly either in favor of the
Pope or of the Councils. Now they speak clearly neither in
favor of the Pope, as the theologians of the Sorbonne show
so splendidly, nor in favor of the Councils, as the theologians of the Pope show so splendidly. We must therefore
conclude that these passages are most obscure. Add to that
the remarks which I have made several times to the effect
that the Gallican church would not dare to treat as heresy
the opinion of those who attribute to the Pope all of the
infallibility promised by Jesus Christ. Neither would the
Pope dare to treat as heresy the opinion of the Gallican
church which attributes this infallibility to the Councils.
We have here an evident proof that the revelation is equally
ambiguous concerning the Councils as it is concerning the
Pope. If the revelation is so ambiguous that neither the
people nor the Pope nor the Councils are capable of determining precisely the seat of this infallible tribunal supposedly established by Jesus Christ, it is clear that the infallibility which the Roman Church arrogates is a vain
imagination. . . . (Chapter 29)

[Bayle found it more difficult to answer the rationalists. He was nonetheless far from being among
their number, for he had made his own pre-Kantian
critique of reason's powers and concluded that purely

rational investigation eventually yielded only antin-
omies, making reason powerless either to affirm or
deny. Here he departs from his editorial impartiality
in answering the arguments of a Socinian book and
declaring against the way of pure reason.]

NEWS OF THE REPUBLIC OF LETTERS, (SEPTEMBER, 1684). RE-
VIEW OF A BOOK ENTITLED "A RATIONAL RELIGION OR
TREATISE ON THE USE OF REASON IN THEOLOGICAL CON-
TROVERSIES," BY ANDREA WISSOWATIUS.

*It is difficult to find a happy medium
between faith and reason.*

We have spoken of this author in the June issue. If we
remember to which sect he belongs [Socinian], we will
understand his intentions simply by looking at the title of
his book. In speaking of the uses of reason in religious matters he broaches a subject in which it is not easy to find a
golden mean, and nonetheless it is necessary to avoid the
two extremes. If reason is entirely excluded from the examination of points of theology, we soon fall into inexplicable difficulties. If we submit all divinely-revealed mysteries to rational scrutiny, we run the risk of explaining
them differently than God wishes. We must therefore take
care, as I have said, to avoid the extremes, but where are
we to find a firm standing ground? If we find it to our
advantage either to exclude or to admit rational examination with regard to certain points, our adversaries use our
same arguments to prove that we must admit it or exclude
it without any restriction when it is to their advantage.

We may very aptly compare faith and reason with sovereigns and subjects. We have seen how difficult it is to find
the mean which regulates the rights of both of them. If you
make the obedience of subjects entirely contingent upon the
examination they make of their prince's orders, you throw
the state into the perpetual danger of civil war. If you give

the prince an unlimited power, you throw the people into the unfortunate necessity of never being able to protect their goods and lives without becoming criminal. It is therefore necessary to avoid both of these extremities. But how are we to do it? In making exceptions we open the gates to the factious who will say that either the exceptions apply to the very points in question or that the very reasons which give us the right to make exceptions to the rule of rational examination, give them the same right also. I advance these points only to show that it is difficult to grant faith and reason their respective rights.

We must agree, moreover, that it is possible to avoid the shoals on each side and that if there are difficulties, they come from a most wise dispensation of God, who, wishing to make us more attentive in the study of His word and to have at the same time proofs of our deference to Him, requires that we exercise our faith and our reason at the same time. The writers of Port Royal make the judicious remark in their treatise upon human faith that "God has not willed that the life of man should be governed by general principles and rules which have no exception. It is false to say that we must never submit. It is false to say that we must always submit, and it is in discerning the occasions in which one must submit and in which one must not submit that we find one of the greatest difficulties of Christian life." However this may be, the book of Wissowatius is not greatly to be feared. He proves only what everyone already grants him, as will appear from the extract we are about to give.

All approaches to religious questions
require the use of reason.

He first states that there are only three possible ways in which to seek a correct understanding of the Scripture. The first is by the decision of a visible and infallible judge. The second is through an individual inspiration given by the Holy Spirit. The third is by the light of reason carefully examining the Holy Scripture. No matter what one does, he says, he must necessarily employ the light of reason. If one uses the first of these ways, it is necessary for either the Pope or the Council to examine the Scripture before rendering a decision, and the Catholics themselves admit that the way in which the Popes and the Councils examine the Word of God when they have to make some decision is not different from the way in which other men examine other things. . . . As far as the individual is concerned, he must make his examination also, because he must not believe in the decision of the Popes or the Councils unless God has established them as judges of the faith. Now in order to know whether or not God has done so, the individual must examine the revealed Word. He must find there that God has left upon the earth a visible and infallible interpreter of his Word. And that is not all—he must search out the characteristics of this interpreter so as to see whether or not they are possessed by the Popes and the Councils, all of which requires a rational examination. With regard to the way of individual inspiration, it is clear that it does not exclude the light of reason because there are fanatics and visionaries who are persuaded that they have the testimony of the Spirit of God in their heart, from which it follows that one must make a choice between an inner testimony and another. Now does not this choice require that one consult, examine, and reason? The author claims that the Jesuit Becanus has shown in his book against Pareus that it is impossible to prove by the testimony of the Holy Spirit that a given meaning is indeed that of the Scripture without arguing in a vicious circle, for it would be necessary afterward to prove by the Scripture that the Holy Spirit bears this testimony. He thus concludes that the three ways of determining the meaning of the Word of God must be reduced to the way of rational examination.

*Reason alone cannot
be the rule of faith.*

All of his labors are to no avail, because he does not touch upon the principal difficulty. Everyone will grant him that examination is necessary. He recognizes himself that the Catholics admit it, and he takes full advantage of their avowal. He should have insisted on some other point if he wished to establish the doctrine of his sect. He should have proved that *reason is so much the rule of our faith that we must believe nothing to be revealed by God that does not conform to the maxims of reason and the experience of nature.* But this is precisely the point which he does not prove and which he will never prove [as I will show]. Thus, his work is of no prejudice to the true doctrine. . . .

In answering the objections raised to him, the author approaches his task like almost all other theologians and philosophers. He answers very fully and exactly all of the weak ones and omits or touches only in passing on those which press him very hard. He has clearly seen that in order to reason consistently with his principles, he must reject as false everything which reason cannot understand. Thus, he denies that God created the world out of nothing. But since he cannot deny that God has existed eternally, another doctrine which is absolutely incomprehensible as to the manner, he escapes in three words and says that our reason agrees very easily to all of that since it shows us that the first of all causes necessarily had no beginning. Anyone who realizes ever so slightly what it is to reason and dispute perceives that the author does not answer this objection. Since reason proves necessarily the existence of something incomprehensible, it follows that there are very true and real things which reason cannot comprehend. As soon as this point is understood, all the arguments which the Socinians draw from the commonplace of incomprehensibility are of no force. The author is perceptive enough to see that his position is not comfortable, and he therefore passes by this question in haste and extends himself upon easy objections such as those concerning miracles, the possibility of which is easily granted by reason. . . .

> [The Protestants, who based their faith upon their examination of the Scripture, had to cope with the questions posed by the textual critics, such as Father Richard Simon, who had shown that there were defects in the Scriptural text. Here Bayle presents a typical Protestant reaction and attempts to shore up this hole in the dike. While still retaining his personal belief in the Scripture, he later realized that textual lapses precluded any infallible way of interpreting it.]

NEWS OF THE REPUBLIC OF LETTERS, JANUARY, 1685. REVIEW OF THE BOOK ENTITLED "EPISTLE FROM ORIGEN TO AMBROSE" CONCERNING A NEW POLYGLOT BIBLE.

*The Scripture is sufficiently perfect
to serve as a rule of faith.*

. . . Mr. Reinier Leers, printer and bookseller of Rotterdam, has shown us several letters from some very learned men in this country, in France, in England, and in Germany, who express great satisfaction concerning the project of printing a new polyglot Bible, and they hope that this project will be brought to fruition as soon as possible. Several among them even congratulated him upon this printing, having believed that he had it in charge. Most of those who have written are good Protestants. But in order to be perfectly candid we must also confess that there are other good Protestants whom this project has alarmed, for suspecting that the author is a Roman Catholic, they imagine that he will be biased and that his work will be distorted by his prejudice. In order for this work to be useful for everyone, they insist, its editor must be as free from bias and party spirit as Adam. We assure the public, and in particular timid scholars, that the author of this polyglot Bible will conduct himself in this manner. Therefore, those among the Protestants who have not approved of the edition of this Bible may put their minds at ease. But there will still be a few of them who will be alarmed because mention will be made of certain supposed errors which have slipped into the Scriptural text.

There is reason to believe, however, that if they enter into the spirit of their Protestant principles and examine this point maturely, they will soon calm their doubts. Indeed, it is not the doctrine of the Protestants that their faith depends upon each book, each chapter, and each verse of the Scripture. Therefore, when someone raises the objection that there are quotations in the Bible which are no longer found, implying that some canonical book has been lost, they do not hesitate to admit that even if that were true, their faith would not be in danger, because the truths necessary to salvation are found clearly enough in that which remains. We can say the same concerning the minor alterations which have allegedly slipped into the Scriptural text. It does not matter whether or not scribes have mistaken one letter for another in various places. The body of revealed truths does not depend on five or six vowels or consonants. It is spread throughout the entire canon, and we find it there unmistakably, even though all of the words are not precisely the same as they were at the beginning. Let us not suppose then that the foundation of our faith depends on an infallible exactness on the part of the scribes and interpreters who were the guardians of the Scripture during two or three thousand years. Neither let us suppose that God never permitted them to mistake one letter for another. For it is as hard to entertain this supposition as it is to believe that the efficacy of the sacraments and our salvation depend on the good intentions of all those who have successively officiated in the holy offices since the time of Jesus Christ. Those who take these things into consideration could never believe that any Protestant would use his influence to oppose the printing of this new polyglot Bible. They feel that they would be furnishing arms to the Roman Catholics if they made the divinity of their religion and all the foundation of their faith contingent upon the incorruptibility of each word in the Scripture. They realize that this procedure could work much mischief, for one could claim that he had completely ruined the faith of this party upon discovering a single alteration in the text of the Bible. The prudence of those in the Roman Church in these matters is to be noted. They would never permit themselves to say that the basis of their faith consists in the infallibility of the Church in matters of fact as well as in matters of ecclesiastical jurisdiction, for after that, nothing would be easier than to destroy the foundation of their faith by pointing out several historical errors of fact made by the Popes and the Councils of the Church.

[In 1684, Nicole, a Jansenist, attempted to put the Protestant-Catholic controversy on a new footing by arguing that even if the first Reformers had been right, they still would not have been justified in separating from the Roman Church, because they could not have had an absolute knowledge that they were right. The effect of his argument was to apply a strict Cartesian criterion to the theological dogmas of religion. In answering Nicole, Bayle concluded that no religious system could satisfy the demands of this rationalism, and he therefore felt it expedient to withdraw from the field. In his view, any religious belief would henceforth have to be founded upon the subjective basis of individual conscience.]

New Critical Letters on "The History of Calvinism"

*The way of authority must be established
by the way of examination.*

I hope that the public will not consider the work of this author unworthy of a reply. He can be answered in two ways: (1) by retorting his arguments; (2) by showing with direct and immediate proofs that common and unlearned people are able to make a choice of a religion without being guilty of a "criminal temerity." The first kind of answer would pose terrible difficulties for Mr. Nicole, because it is useless for him to claim that his principles permit the unlearned of the Catholic Church to substitute the judgment of the Church for their own—he will still need to show how they can be sure that they do well in relying upon the examination rendered by the Church. They will be culpable of a "criminal temerity" if they are not legitimately assured that this substitution is right, necessary, and sufficient, and that their own examination is illegitimate, useless, insufficient, and superfluous. Now how can the common, simple, and unlearned members of the Roman Church be assured of all of that? Does Mr. Nicole propose that they acquire this assurance by the way of reason? But he tells us that there are people "who should be condemned for the very fact that they reason, because when one has to do with those questions and practices which depend only upon authority, it is assuredly faulty to attempt to decide them by reasoning." Is not the question under discussion here of this kind? Does it not depend completely upon the will of God? It is therefore necessary to consult the Scripture and the tradition of the Church in order to know if the unlearned should substitute the judgment of the Church for their own. The unlearned must therefore be assured by the written and unwritten word of God upon all of the points which I have marked. How will they do this better than the unlearned of our own Communion? And so here we see the difficulty re-torted. The remark which I have made previously is appro-priate here—in the time of Luther and Calvin all of the Christians of the West found themselves equally obliged to reflect upon their belief and to see whether they should remain as they were or whether they should embrace the new religion. Those of both parties needed to examine their principles. Those in favor of the Reformation had to exam-ine the accusations leveled at them by the Communion of Rome. Those who continued in the religion where they were born had to examine at least why they should not examine each article and why they should depend upon the judgments of the prelates of Trent.

The effect of religious controversy

But to state my thought ingenuously I would not want to see Mr. Nicole answered only by retortion, because if we did no more than that, we would only augment the danger of the arms which he has unconsciously furnished to the libertines and the Deists, or to those who believe that one can be saved in all Christian societies and that we should thus continue to live in the one in which we were born or else accept the one which enjoys the most favorable circum-stances in the world. These arms, I say, which he has fur-nished to these people would remain in their hands with a renewed force. This is why. They would say, "The Catholics show very well that the Protestants have no legitimate cer-tainty of their belief, but the Protestants cast the Catholics on the same rock. Consequently, it is impossible to be assured of the revealed truth. There is therefore no other choice to make than to remain where we are or always to be a part of the dominant religion." You see that it is ex-tremely important to disarm that group by proving directly that the unlearned of our religion can attain to a legitimate certainty of a celestial truth.

Conscience must be the rule of faith.

To prove it sufficiently we must establish this principle, that *in questions of religion one must not wait until he has acquired all of the evidence asked for in the philosophy of Mr. Descartes before making a decision and consenting to believe.*

In order to establish this principle we must pose a second, something like this, that *in questions of religion the standard of judgment is not in the understanding but in the conscience,* that is, we must receive objects not according to the clear and distinct ideas acquired by a severe examination, but according to the dictates of our conscience by which we feel that in accepting them we will do what is pleasing before God. We must necessarily come to this point. The faith which the Holy Spirit instills in us fills us with a full persuasion without the aid of a long examination. On the other hand, if we wished to depend only upon the light of understanding, we could not accept the dogmas of a religion without having observed all of the precepts of Mr. Descartes. Now this undertaking surpasses the capabilities of almost all Christians, and if it were necessary, there would not be two Christians out of ten thousand who could maintain their belief except by a "criminal temerity."

I would not even except those persecutors of the early Christians who, upon seeing the constancy of our martyrs, abandoned their office of executioner in order to share immediately in the glorious crown of martyrdom. I maintain that the faith which God communicated to them by the sight of these great objects did not enlighten their reason in the way that Mr. Descartes requires in order to avoid a rash consent. If these executioners had wished to act strictly according to the Cartesian spirit, they would have had to reason thus: "It is better to die with those who suffer for a truth which God Himself has revealed than to live. Now these Christians suffer for a truth which God Himself has revealed. Therefore, it is better to die with these Christians than to live."

The major premise of this syllogism is very easy to understand, but the minor premise requires much debate if we wish to make a Cartesian examination of it before believing it. For this proposition to possess Cartesian evidence it is necessary to know whether the constancy shown by these martyrs could have had any other cause than the firm persuasion of a truth revealed by God Himself. In order to verify this proposition, we must know at least two things thoroughly: (1) that during all the time that there have been men in the world, there has not been one who for human motives endured death with as much constancy as did the martyrs of Christianity; (2) that man is not capable of suffering with such constancy if he is not suffering for a truth which God has revealed to him.

It is quite certain that an executioner of the early martyrs who himself became a martyr on the spot did not know either of these two things. He did not have the time to look through all recorded history. The history books did not report all of the examples of constancy. They did not explain the secret workings of the heart, and as for the nature of man, it is an abyss of such infinite capacity that only God knows all of its extent. The combinations of temperament, passion, and prejudice can vary in so many more ways than we are capable of knowing, that it would be foolish to say, "Such and such a thing had never before happened to any man; therefore, it has not happened to any man today." And do we know all of the ways in which our soul depends upon spiritual beings? Do we know all of the caprices of spirits more powerful than ours? It is therefore certain that these Christians who were converted in an instant did not know the two things which I mentioned, and they nonetheless believed in the Gospel in the way most holy and pleasing before God and the most exempt from rashness. Therefore, the conviction of the Christians does not require this philosophic research without which our understanding is guilty of temerity even when it assents to true objects.

Let no one object that the faith of these converted executioners was so keen that it gave them more knowledge than they could have acquired by thirty years of study. All Christians agree that even though faith fills us with a complete assurance (a certainty more firm than that furnished by geometry) it does not give us the same reasons for certainty which human knowledge uses to support its demonstration. All Christians agree that faith does not make up for the lack of knowledge in matters of fact. No one maintains that in order to be sure of a revealed truth, one needs to understand the original languages of the Scripture, for otherwise no one would ever be a faithful Christian without having studied Greek and Hebrew. Consequently, we may assume that these executioners who became martyrs did not receive a faith which had the same effect upon them as the study of history. From this it follows that at the moment of their martyrdom they had no more knowledge of what had happened in the world than they had had just before their conversion. . . .

I will not enter further into this question which appears to me too fraught with difficulties for someone who has already finished his book and writes this only by way of a postscript. Some people will perhaps tell me that the question appears very difficult to me because of the smallness of my mind. They will be right. I would therefore be very happy for some accomplished person to cast more light upon this fine subject and to show, if he can, that in matters of religion we are, through the providence of God, led by reason and not by instinct, as we are often led in other matters. It has been said that the principal concern of a rich man is not to know how he became rich, but to be rich. Cannot we say the same of faith? Whether faith enters into our mind by our education, or by our prejudices, or by chance, or by reasonings, the most important thing is to possess it. . . . (Postscript to Chapter XI of original work)

Chapter III

REASON AND TOLERANCE

[During 1685–1686 the persecution of the French Protestants became increasingly severe. (Bayle's own brother, a pastor, died of treatment received at the hands of Catholic converters). Catholic apologists maintained that they were simply bringing the erring sheep back into the fold, and they cited the Parable of the Great Supper to justify their conduct. Did not the master command his servants "to go out into the highways and hedges and compel them to come in, that my house may be filled?" (Luke 14:23) Had not St. Augustine cited the same parable to justify the use of force against the heretic Donatists in the fourth century A.D.?

When Bayle, filled with indignation, undertook to refute any possible justification of intolerance, the emphasis of his thought shifted from the defense of theological doctrines to the critique of moral practices. Without extending his principle to the dogmas of the faith, he now insisted on the necessity of interpreting the Scripture rationally, for even if reason could not always tell what was true in speculative questions, it could at least tell what was not true in matters of moral practice. The effect of his answer, the *Philosophic Commentary,* was first to exalt reason by showing its beneficent results in practical matters and to abase faith by demonstrating the impossibility of ascertaining the truth of abstract dogmas.]

A Philosophic Commentary upon These Words of Jesus Christ: "Compel Them to Come In," Whereby It Is Proved by Many Demonstrative Reasons That Nothing Is More Abominable Than to Make Conversions by Force, and Also the Apology Which St. Augustine Made of Persecutions

Natural light, or the general principles of knowledge, is the basic and primitive standard of all interpretation of the Scripture, especially with regard to morals.

I leave it to the theologians and the textual critics to explicate this passage by examining what precedes and what follows, by showing the force of the terms of the original, and of their various possible meanings, and of the meanings which they indeed do have in several places in the Scripture. As for myself, I aspire to write a new kind of commentary and to found it upon principles which are more general and more infallible than anything which the study of languages and criticisms and commonplaces could furnish me. I will not even try to discover why Jesus Christ used this expression *compel*, nor will I try to ascertain its legitimate meaning, nor will I try to discover whether there be some mystery lurking beneath its surface. I will limit myself to refuting the literal meaning which the persecutors give to it.

In order to refute it incontrovertibly I will base my argument upon this principle of natural light, that any literal meaning which entails the obligation to commit crimes is false. St. Augustine himself sets down this rule for discerning between the figurative meaning and the literal meaning of the Scripture. Jesus Christ, he tells us, declares that if we do not eat the flesh of the Son of Man, we will not be saved. It seems that this interpretation enjoins us to commit a crime. These words must therefore be taken as a figure which enjoins us to participate in Communion and to bring to our remembrance for our edification that the Lord's flesh was crucified and wounded for us. This is not the place to examine whether or not these words prove that St. Augustine was not of the opinion of the Roman Church, or whether or not he applies his own rule appropriately. Suffice it to say that he bases his reasoning upon this fundamental principle of Scriptural exegesis that *if a literal interpretation of the Scripture obliges men to commit crimes* or (to be perfectly clear) to perform acts which natural light, the precepts of the Decalogue, and the morality of the Gospel prohibit, we must assuredly conclude that its proponents have given the Scripture a false meaning, and instead of a divine revelation, they offer us nothing more than their own imaginations, passions, or prejudices.

The necessity of a rational criterion

Far be it from me to wish to extend the jurisdiction of natural light and the principles of metaphysics as far as do the Socinians, who reject any meaning given to the Scripture which does not conform to this light and these principles and who because of this maxim refuse to believe the doctrines of the Trinity and the Incarnation. No, I do not believe that this maxim is without limits, [but] I know full well that there are axioms against which the most express and evident words of the Scripture would be powerless, as for example, the whole is greater than its parts; if from equal parts one takes away equal parts, the remainders are equal; it is impossible for two contradictory statements both to be true; or that the essence of a subject continues really to subsist after the destruction of the subject. Even if one were to show a hundred Scriptural passages contradicting these propositions, even if one were to perform thousands upon thousands of miracles, more than Moses and the Apostles, in order to establish a doctrine opposed to these universal maxims of common sense, people would still not be convinced. Rather, they would be persuaded either that the Scripture spoke only by metaphor or that these miracles came from the devil, for they cannot believe that the natural light of men which dictates these maxims is deceptive.

Theologians pay homage to reason.

Those of the Roman Church are so convinced of this fact that even as ready as they are to sacrifice their metaphysics and to render suspect all the principles of common sense, they nonetheless recognize that neither the Scripture, nor the Church, nor miracles can prevail against the clear light of reason. For example . . . all the controversialists of the Catholic party deny that transubstantiation is contrary to sound philosophy and they invent endless distinctions and subtleties in order to show that they are not ruining the principles of metaphysics. Likewise, the Protestants, when they are disputing with the Socinians, will not grant that the doctrines of the Trinity and the Incarnation are self-contradictory. They maintain and they prove that no one can show them how these doctrines are contradictory. Thus, all theologians of whatever party they may be, can talk as much as they wish of the merits of faith, the compelling force of revelation, and the profundity of the mysteries, but after all is said and done they come humbly to pay homage at the foot of the throne of reason. They recognize, although they do not say it in so many words (but their conduct is sufficiently expressive and eloquent), that the Supreme Tribunal from which there is no appeal is reason speaking through the axioms of natural light, or of metaphysics.

Let us therefore be done with the idea that theology is a queen and that philosophy is her servant. The theologians themselves give evidence by their conduct that they regard philosophy as the queen and theology as the servant, for the source of all of their intellectual gymnastics is the desire not to be in contradiction with sound philosophy. Rather than so expose themselves they change their principles of philosophy, de-emphasizing this one or that one according to their particular need. But by all of these procedures they recognize clearly the superiority of philosophy and the essential need which they feel of its approval. They would not go to so much trouble to conform to its laws if they did not recognize that any dogma which is not, so to speak, confirmed, verified, and recorded by the Supreme Parliament of reason and natural light can be of only a very uncertain authority and fragile as glass.

The universality of the rational criterion

The reason for their conduct is not difficult to find. When we perceive that a keen and distinct light enlightens all men as soon as they open the eyes of their understanding and that this light convinces them fully of its truth, we must conclude that it is God Himself, the essential and substantial Truth, who enlightens us immediately and permits us to contemplate in their essence the ideas of eternal truths contained in the principles of metaphysics. Now why would God do so with respect to all of these individual truths, why would He thus reveal them in all ages to all peoples of the earth and not leave people the freedom to doubt them? Why, I ask, would He conduct Himself thus, if it were not in order to give us a standard and a criterion of the other ideas which are continually presented to us and which are partly true and partly false, partly obscure and partly clear? God foresaw that because of the laws governing the union of the soul and body, the Divine Essence could not infallibly reveal to man all kinds of truths and thus to keep him from error. He nonetheless desired to endow the soul with a sure means of discerning truth from error, and that means is natural light, or the principles of metaphysics, by which we can determine the soundness or falsity of the individual doctrines of our books or teachers. It follows therefore that we cannot be assured of the veracity of anything unless this thing agrees with this primitive and universal light which God sheds forth upon the souls of all men, convincing them infallibly and invincibly as soon as they give heed to it. It is by this original and metaphysical light that people have been able to discern the true meaning of endless passages of Scripture which, if taken according to the literal and popular meaning of the words, would have thrown us into the grossest ideas concerning the Godhead.

I say once again, far be it from me to wish to extend this principle as far as do the Socinians. But if it has certain limitations with respect to speculative truths, I do not think that it should have any with respect to practical and general principles which concern morals. I mean that without exception we must submit all moral laws to this natural idea of justice, which just as metaphysic light, "enlightens every man who comes into the world."

Reason must be abstracted from custom and personal interest.

But if a man really desires to understand these ideas of natural justice or equity, I would ask him to consider them in general, divorcing them from his own personal interest and the customs of his country, for passions and prejudices obscure only too often our ideas of natural justice. When a man looks upon an action as very useful and agreeable for himself, he may easily be persuaded by a subtle and deeply-rooted prejudice that this action is reasonable. It is also possible that the strength of custom and the peculiar stamp given to the soul by early education will lead one to believe that a certain act is blameless when, in reality, it is not. Therefore, if one wishes to overcome these two obstacles and to ascertain the dictates of natural light concerning morality, I would ask him first to hold himself aloof from his own personal interest and the manners of his country and then to ask himself this question: If a certain custom were to be introduced into a country where it had not been in usage, would it be worthy of acceptance after a free and critical examination? I believe that this abstraction would dispel many of the clouds which sometimes come between our minds and this pure and universal light which emanates from God to make known to all men the general principles of equity, this light which is the touchstone of all precepts and individual laws, for I do not except even those which God has subsequently revealed to us extraordinarily, either by speaking to us Himself or by sending us His inspired prophets.

Even Adam was guided principally by natural light.

I am persuaded that before Adam heard any audible voice telling him what he should do, God had already spoken to him inwardly by causing him to perceive the grandeur and immensity of the idea of the sovereignly perfect Being and of the eternal laws of all that is right and just. This being so, Adam did not believe himself obliged to obey God so much because a certain prohibition had fallen upon his ears as because the inner light which had instructed him even before God spoke to him, continued to make known to him his duty and his dependence upon the Supreme Being. Thus, even with regard to Adam it will be found true that the revealed truth was submitted, as it were, to the natural light of reason to be verified, registered, approved, and to receive its status as a law. . . .

Since the Fall it has been even more necessary for men to depend on natural light.

But if Adam before his fall verified the authenticity of the verbal prohibition pronounced by God by comparing it with the idea which he already had of the Supreme Being, it became even more imperative for him to do so afterward, when he had become aware that two kinds of angels were attempting to tell him what he should or should not do. It became indispensable for him to have a standard of discernment, so as not to confuse what God would apparently reveal to him with what the devil, disguised under dazzling appearances, might advise or order him to do. And this standard could be nothing else than natural light, that is, the feeling of justice and righteousness imprinted upon the souls of all men. It is, in a word, that universal reason which enlightens all minds and which never fails those who consult it attentively, especially in those lucid intervals when the mind is not occupied with thought of corporeal objects or troubled by passions which have been excited in the heart. All the dreams and visions of the patriarchs, all of the messages which fell upon their ears as coming from God, all apparitions of angels, all miracles, everything in general had to be submitted to the scrutiny of natural light. Otherwise, how would one have known if these manifestations came from the source of evil which had deceived Adam, or from the Creator of all things? To everything that came from Him, God had to give a certain stamp which agreed with, or at least did not contradict, the natural light which is communicated immediately to all minds, whereupon people willingly received the individual laws of Moses or some other prophet as coming from God. . . .

Therefore, if the natural and metaphysical light, if the general principles of knowledge, if these primitive ideas which carry in themselves their own persuasion, have been given to us so that we may judge things correctly, they must be our sovereign arbiters. We must submit *all our differences upon obscure points* to their decision. It follows that if someone takes it into his head to claim that God has revealed a precept of morality which is in direct contradiction with these basic principles, we must deny his precept. We must answer that he is advancing a false meaning and that it is much more appropriate for him to reject the testimony of his textual criticism and his grammar than that of reason.

If we do not come to this point, good-bye to all of our faith, according to the remark of the worthy Father Valerian. "If someone," he says, "insists that we must make our understanding bow to faith to the point of calling nature's standard of judgment into question, or even of believing it false in certain cases, I say that by that very insistence he necessarily destroys faith. It is absolutely impossible to believe anything at all without reasoning that He in whom we believe is deceiving neither us nor Himself, and this reasoning obviously is worthless without the natural standard of judging which has been explained heretofore."

The Catholic writers must also
dispute upon rational grounds.

This is the terminal point of all Roman Catholic writings against the way of reason and in favor of the authority of the Church. Without being aware of it, they only make a large circle and come back after much labor and fatigue to the point where the others go immediately. The others say frankly and without wasting words that we must hold to the meaning which appears to us to be the best. The Catholics, on the other hand, say that we must take care not to do so because our individual lights can deceive us. Our reason is only darkness and illusion, they say, and we must therefore defer to the judgment of the Church. But is this not coming back to reason? If one prefers the judgment of the Church to his own, does he not make the decision by virtue of this reasoning: the Church is more enlightened than I am; therefore, it is more believable than I am? It is consequently the individual's own enlightenment which determines the course to follow. If he believes that something is revealed, it is because his common sense, his natural light, and his reason tell him that the proofs offered of the revelation are sound.

But where will one be if he must distrust his reason as a dark and deceptive principle? Must he not then distrust his reason even when it tells him that "the Church is more enlightened than I am and therefore more believable than I am?" Must he not then fear that his reason is deceived both as to the principle and the conclusion derived from it? And what will one do also with this argument? "All that God says is true. Now God says by Moses that He created a first man. Therefore, that is true." If we do not have a natural light to serve as an infallible rule by which to judge of everything that is called into question (including the question of whether a given idea is contained in the Scripture), will we not have reason to doubt the major premise of this argument and by consequence the conclusion? And because we would then find ourselves on the path to the most dreadful chaos and the most detestable skepticism imaginable, we must necessarily come to this conclusion: any individual dogma, whether it is said to be contained in the Scripture or whether it is otherwise advanced, is false when refuted by the clear and distinct ideas of natural light, and principally with respect to morality. (Part I, Chapter I)

First refutation of the literal meaning of these words "Compel them to come in," by the reason that it is opposed by the most distinct ideas of natural light.

I have felt obliged to my readers to establish the universality of the foregoing principles, but now I come to the particular subject and the specific matter of my commentary on these words of the passage "Compel them to come in," and this is how I reason: the literal meaning of these words is contrary to the most distinct ideas which reason teaches us; therefore, it is false.

Purely external acts cannot please God.

It is no longer a question of proving the antecedent, for I believe that I have sufficiently proved this point in the first chapter. I will then say that (1) we know by the clearest and most distinct ideas of reason that there is a sovereignly perfect Being who governs all things, who is to be worshipped by man, who approves and rewards certain actions, and who disapproves and punishes others; (2) we know in the same way that the principal worship which man offers to this Being consists of acts of the mind. If the wind blows over a statue as the king passes by or if the king sees marionettes on their knees, we cannot imagine that he would consider these postures as marks of homage rendered to him. How much more must we believe that God, who judges infallibly of all things, does not account any purely external motion as an act of submission and worship? We must therefore say that all external acts of religion, all the expenditures for sacrifices, altars, and temples are accepted of God only inasmuch as they are accompanied by inward acts of the soul.

It follows very clearly that the essence of religion consists in the judgment which our minds form of God and in the respect, fear, and love which our will feels for Him. It is therefore even possible for a man to fulfill his duty toward God without any external act. But since these cases are not usual, we would do better to say that the inward disposition which constitutes the essence of religion manifests itself outwardly by gestures of humility and by signs which make known the honor which the soul renders to the majesty of God. Whatever the case may be, it is nonetheless true that the outward signs made by a man who feels nothing for God (one who has neither the views nor the will which he should have with respect to God) are no more an honor to God than the overturning of a statue by a chance gust of wind.

Force cannot produce true religion.

It is then clear that the only legitimate way to inspire religion is to produce within the soul certain views and acts of will concerning God. Now since threats, persecutions, fines, exiles, beatings, tortures, and generally everything that is contained in the literal meaning of constraint cannot create these acts of will which constitute the essence of religion, it is clear that this use of constraint to establish a religion is false. Consequently, Jesus Christ did not command it.

I do not deny that the use of force produces within the soul certain views and acts of will, in addition to the external postures which are the usual signs of inward religion. These attitudes, however, are not toward God, but only toward the originators of the constraint. The persecuted judge that their persecutors are to be feared, and they indeed fear them. But those people who did not have the proper views concerning God beforehand and did not feel due respect, love, and fear for Him, do not acquire these ideas and feelings when someone forces them to go through the outward forms of religion. Likewise, those who held certain ideas of God beforehand and who believed that He was to be honored only in a certain way which was different than that of the persecutors, do not change their inward feeling toward God either. Their only new thoughts are to fear their persecutors and to retain their goods which are in danger. Thus, these manifestations of force accomplish nothing with respect to God, for the inward acts they produce have no relationship to Him. And as for the outward acts, it is evident that they are accepted by God only as they are accompanied by the inward dispositions of the soul which are the essence of religion. This should be sufficient to assure the solidity of this proof.

The nature of religion is a certain persuasion of the soul with regard to God which produces in the will the feelings of love, respect, and fear which this Supreme Being deserves, and in the members of the body the signs appropriate to this persuasion and disposition of the will. Therefore, if the outward signs are accompanied by an inappropriate or contradictory disposition of the soul, they are acts of hypocrisy, bad faith, or infidelity and revolt against conscience. . . .

To try to convert people by force to a religion they do not profess is consequently in evident contradiction with common sense and natural light, the general principles of reason, and, in a word, with the original and basic rule of discerning the true from the false, the good from the bad. The clear and distinct ideas which we have of the essence of certain things persuade us invincibly that God cannot reveal to us anything which contradicts them. (For example, we are entirely certain that God cannot reveal that the whole is smaller than its parts; that it is proper to prefer vice to virtue; that we should esteem our dog above our friend and our country; that to go from one place to another by sea we should start out at a gallop on a horse; that in order to prepare a field for an abundant harvest we must not cultivate it.) It is then evident that God has not commanded us in His word to force acceptance of the Gospel upon people by means of beatings or other such violences. Thus, if we find in the Gospel a passage which commands us to do the contrary, we may be assured that the meaning is figurative and not literal, just as if we found in the Scripture a passage which commanded us to become very learned in languages and all kinds of capabilities without studying, we would believe that this passage should be understood figuratively, or that the passage had been falsified, or that we did not understand all of the meanings of the terms in the original, or that it is a mystery which speaks of a people unlike ourselves who are to come after us. Finally, we might believe it to be a precept given according to the oriental way of speaking, that is, by emblems, symbols, and obscure images. We would believe anything rather than be persuaded that God, wise as He is, commanded men literally and properly to acquire a profound knowledge without study. . . . (Part I, Chapter II)

> [Bayle gives eight other refutations of the literal meaning of the parable—violence is contrary to the spirit of the Gospel; it makes vice indistinguishable from virtue; it furnishes the infidels with a very plausible excuse for refusing to let Christian missionaries enter their domains, since Christians would obviously attempt to spread their belief by force; it inevitably leads to the commission of crimes; it would deprive the Christians of the arguments they use against the Mohammedans who spread their religion by the sword; it was unknown to the early Fathers of the Church; it would nullify the protestations of the early Christians, who believed themselves unjustly persecuted; and it would continually expose the true Christians, whoever they might be, to persecution, since each sect believes itself orthodox and would feel obliged to persecute all others which were weaker than itself. Then, after answering several possible objections to his arguments, Bayle finds difficulties which he felt to be more cogent and pressing.]

The obscurity of human knowledge

Among the numerous infirmities of man is this, that he knows truth only imperfectly. If he can prove a thing by clear and demonstrative *a priori* reasons, his joy is soon spoiled by the absurd or at least troublesome consequences which people claim will derive from his conclusion. And if he is fortunate enough not to be overwhelmed by reductions *ad absurdum* (the absurdities which follow from his idea) he has the mortification of having only obscure ideas and weak proofs of what he maintains. (Those who defend either the infinite divisibility of matter or the atoms of Epicurus will know what I am talking about.) I have enough good faith to admit that if my idea has a weak side, it is in its consequences. The direct proofs in my favor are marvelous. The consequences of the opposite idea are monstrous. So far so good, but when one looks upon the practical results of my hypothesis, things no longer go so smoothly. One would say that in order to humiliate our mind, God does not want it to find a standing ground too easily and sets traps for it on all sides. I nonetheless have the advantage that all of the supposedly fearful consequences of my hypothesis can be resolved, as you will see presently.

The political evils caused by religion are due to intolerance.

It is commonly said that there is no more dangerous plague in a state than the multiplicity of religions, because it causes dissension between friends and neighbors, fathers and children, husbands and wives, and sovereigns and subjects. I answer that far from working against me, this argument is a very strong proof in favor of tolerance. If a multiplicity of religions is harmful to a state, it is only because one religion does not wish to tolerate another and sets out to crush it by persecution. *Hinc prima mali labes*, this is the source of the evil. If each religion practiced the tolerance which I advocate, a state divided by ten religions would enjoy the same peace and harmony as a city where all the different kinds of artisans live together in peace in spite of their differences. The only result of religious toleration would be an honest effort on the part of each sect to distinguish itself by its piety, its virtuous acts, and its learning. Each one would make it a matter of pride to show by its good works that it was the most favored of God. Each would even show forth more devotion to the state if the sovereign protected all of them and judged them all with equity. Now such an honest emulation among them would obviously be the source of an infinite amount of good, and consequently nothing would be more apt to restore the Golden Age than toleration. Certainly the harmony which it would establish among several voices and instruments of varying tones and keys would not be any less pleasing than the uniformity of a single voice. But what stands in the way of this fine concert of diverse voices and sounds? It is the desire of one of the religions to exercise a cruel tyranny over the minds of others and to force others to sacrifice their consciences. It is the unjust partiality of kings who deliver the executive power of the state over to the raging and tumultuous desires of a populace of monks and religionists. In a word, all the strife comes not from tolerance, but from intolerance. . . . (Part II, Chapter VI)

[After answering other objections, Bayle examines the contention that the orthodox have the right to force heretics to accept the truth. Bayle answers that even the "erring conscience" of a heretic must be respected because there is no way of infallibly determining the truth of the abstract dogmas of religion.]

There is no sure mark of abstract truth.

If you ask a man to do any more [than to follow his conscience], it is clear that you are asking him to fix his love and zeal only upon the absolute truth, infallibly recognized as such. Now in our present human condition it is impossible for us to know with certainty that that which appears to us to be truth is in fact the absolute truth. (I am speaking here of the particular truths of religion, and not of the properties of numbers, nor of the first principles of metaphysics, nor of the maxims of geometry.) Indeed, all we can do is to be fully persuaded that we possess the absolute truth, that we are not mistaken, and that our opponents are mistaken. But this persuasion is an equivocal mark of the truth since it is found in the most hopelessly lost heretics. It is therefore certain that it is impossible for us to find any sure sign by which we might discern our true ideas, which we believe to be true, from our false ideas, which we also believe to be true. It is not by Cartesian evidence that we can make this discernment, because, to the contrary, everyone says that the truths which God reveals to us in His Word are profound mysteries which require us to make our understanding bow to faith. It is not by incomprehensibility that we can know the truth—what is there more false and at the same time more incomprehensible than a square circle, than a Supreme Being who is essentially evil, or a god which begets offspring by carnal generation, such as the Jupiter of paganism? It is not by the satisfaction of one's conscience, for a papist is as satisfied with his religion, a Turk with his, and a Jew with his, as we are with ours. It is not by the courage and zeal which an opinion produces, for false religions have their martyrs, their unbelievable austerities, a spirit of proselyting greater than the charity of the orthodox, and an extreme attachment to their superstitious ceremonies. In a word, there is nothing by which one can recognize the truth or falsity of his conviction. Thus, if you require that he discern infallibly between truth and error, you ask him to do more than he is able. All that he can do is to say that certain things appear false to him after examination and others true. We must therefore ask him to try to make true objects appear to be true to him. But whether he succeeds or whether he still mistakes error for truth, he must then abide by what he believes to be true. . . .

Ever since the Protestants left the Roman Church, they have constantly heard the objection that in rejecting the authority of the Church, they attempt to find the truth by examination of the Scripture and that this examination is beyond the means of an individual. . . . We complain about this argument being brought up again and again after we have answered it a thousand times, and yet we must admit that the Catholic writers are right in a certain way in continuing to bring it up, because it is not answered and cannot be answered without making the usual supposition that God requires each individual to know the absolute truth and to know that he knows it. Let us admit the debt: neither the learned nor the ignorant can attain such certainty by the way of examination. This way will never lead us to the criterion of truth, which is an idea so clear and distinct that after having considered all of the reasons to doubt we still feel keenly that it cannot be otherwise. It is not possible to arrive at such an idea with regard to this one point of fact, that a given passage of Scripture has been translated correctly, that the Word which is in Greek or Hebrew today has always been there; and that the meaning given it by the interpreters, the commentators, and the translators is the one intended by the author of the book. We can have a moral certainty of it, based upon very great probabilities. But in the final analysis, this certainty can be found in a multitude of people who are mistaken. Thus, it is not a sure mark of truth. It is not what is called a *criterium veritatis*, which is the irresistible evidence by which we know, for example, that the whole is greater than its parts; that if from equal things one subtracts equal portions, the remainders are equal; that six is half of twelve, etc. . . .

[Bayle here repeats his contention that the Catholics are vulnerable to the same objections which they raise to the Protestants. He then continues:]

God does not require man
to find the absolute truth.

If you weigh these ideas carefully and meditate upon them profoundly you will no doubt see that the truth which I am attempting to establish here is that man in his present condition is required by God only to seek the truth as carefully as he can and, believing to have found it, to love it and take it for his guide. As everyone can see, this is a proof that we are obliged to have the same attitude toward the apparent truth as for the real truth. When this point is accepted, all the objections which are raised concerning the difficulty of individual examination disappear as mirages— it is certain that each individual, no matter how simple, is able to give a meaning to what he reads, or to what is read to him, and to feel that this meaning is true, and he then possesses his own truth. It is sufficient for each individual to consult sincerely and in good faith the light which God gives him, and after that to commit himself to the idea which seems the most reasonable and consistent with the will of God. If he does that, he is orthodox with respect to God, although by an unavoidable defect his thoughts may not be a faithful image of the reality of things, just as a child is orthodox in taking the husband of his mother to be his father, although he may not really be his son. The most important consideration is thereafter to act virtuously, and thus, each one must employ all of his means in honoring God by a prompt obedience to the precepts of morality. And as for the knowledge of our duties in questions of conduct, the revealed light is so clear that few people go astray when they seek it in good faith. (Part II, Chapter X)

[Bayle devotes Part III of the *Philosophic Commentary* to analyzing and refuting the specific arguments which St. Augustine had advanced to justify the use of force to make the Donatists return to the orthodox fold.]

Chapter IV

REASON AND EVIL

[Of all of the challenges offered both to the Christian faith and to the new rationalism, the problem of evil was the most formidable. Articles in his *Historical and Critical Dictionary* on the two ancient heretical sects of the Manicheans and the Paulicians gave Bayle the opportunity to set forth the sum of his thought on this subject. The effect of these, and other articles, was to pronounce a complete divorce of faith and reason.

Bayle divided each of the articles in his *Dictionary* into a short text, containing introductory remarks, and voluminous notes, containing amplification of his views or erudition. The entire text is presented here first and is followed by the notes in order.]

Manicheans. Heretics, whose infamous sect was founded by a certain Manes (A) in the third century A.D. It became established in several provinces and subsisted for a long time. Nonetheless, they taught such doctrines as ought to cause us the greatest horror. Their weakness did not consist, as one might think at first, in the dogma of two principles [i.e., first causes], one good and the other evil, but in the detailed explanations that they gave of them and in the practical consequences derived from them (B). It must be admitted that this false doctrine, which is much more ancient than Manes (C) and indefensible as soon as one admits the Holy Scriptures either in whole or in part, would be quite difficult to refute if it were defended by pagan philosophers well trained in the art of disputation (D). It was fortunate that St. Augustine, who was so well versed in all of the skills of controversy, abandoned his

Manicheanism, for he would have been capable of rejecting the grossest errors of the system and constructing a system which in his hands would have caused great difficulty to the orthodox. Pope Leo I showed much vigor against the Manicheans, and since his zeal was supported by the imperial laws, (E) this sect received a very rude blow at that time [ca. 439 A.D.]. It became formidable in Armenia in the ninth century, as I explain elsewhere [in the article "Paulicians"], and appeared in France at the time of the Albigensians. These facts are undeniable, but it is not true that the Albigensians were Manicheans. The latter taught, among other errors, that the souls of plants are rational, and they condemned agriculture as a murderous occupation. But they permitted their hearers to practice it in favor of the elect (F).

*Remark A. Sect founded by a
certain Manes. . . .*

[Bayle here gives a brief biography of Manes.]

*Remark B. . . . the practical
consequences derived from them*

According to the Manicheans, the two principles gave battle to one another, and during this conflict a mixture of good and evil was produced. Henceforth, the good principle endeavored to separate what belonged to Him and spread His power among the elements to bring about this separation. The elect aided in the endeavor, for all that was impure in the meat that they ate, separated from the particles of the good principle, and then these particles, when severed and purified, were transported to the kingdom of God, their first country, in two vessels appointed for that purpose. These two vessels are the sun and moon. These heretics "imagined that to save souls, God had made a great machine composed of twelve vessels which gradually carried the souls upward until it unloaded them on the moon, which, having purified these souls by its rays, conveyed them into the sun and into glory. It was thus that they explained the different appearances of the moon. It was in the full when the vessels arrived there bearing a multitude of souls, and it decreased in proportion as these souls were removed out of it into glory." [1] There were in these vessels, they said, certain Powers which assumed the shape of a man, to entice the women of the other party to fall in love with them, so that the fires of lust would reciprocally separate the substances of light from the substances of darkness. If you add to this, that they imagined the parts of light to be much more intermixed with the parts of darkness in people during the act of procreation than at other times, you may understand the monstrous alliance they made between these two doctrines, for they concluded that men must neither marry nor procreate children, but could give free rein to the transports of nature, provided they hindered conception. . . .

Remark C. This false dogma, much more ancient than Manes . . .

[Bayle shows that the belief in two Principles was sometimes held among the ancient Greeks and Romans.]

Remark D. It would be very difficult to refute the Manichean doctrine if it were defended by pagan philosophers who were well trained in the art of disputation.

By *a priori* reasons they would have been quickly bested, but in *a posteriori* reasons they excelled. Here you

[1] [Basnage, *History of the Religion of the Reformed Churches, tome I*, pp. 125–126. Bayle draws all his other information on the Manicheans from St. Augustine's treatise *Upon Heretics*. Ed. note]

could have fought against them for a long time, and it would have been difficult to gain any advantage over them. I can better make myself understood by the explanation which follows.

Our clearest and most certain ideas of order teach us that a necessary, eternal, and self-existent Being must be one, infinite, almighty, and endowed with all kinds of perfections. Thus, if we consult only these ideas we find nothing more absurd than the hypothesis of two eternal and independent principles, one of which is not only bereft of goodness but is able to frustrate the purposes of the other. That is what I call *a priori* reasons. They lead us necessarily to reject this hypothesis and to admit only one principle of all things.

If only *a priori* reasons were needed in order to establish the soundness of a system, the dispute would be quickly settled to the confusion of Zoroaster and all of his followers. But in order for any system to be sound it needs two things: (1) its ideas must be distinct; and (2) it must account for what experience teaches us. We must therefore see whether or not the phenomena of nature can be conveniently explained by the hypothesis of a single principle. When the Manicheans maintain that the existence of contrary qualities in the world (cold and heat, white and black, light and darkness) implies necessarily the existence of two first principles, their argument is pitiful. The opposition which we find between these qualities, no matter how much it is supported by the variations, disorders, and irregularities of nature, cannot constitute half an objection to the unity, the simplicity, and the immutability of God. We can explain all of these things either by the various faculties which God has given to material bodies, or by the laws of movement which He has established, or by the concurrence of intelligent occasional causes, by which He was pleased to act. We do not need to have recourse to the quintessences which certain rabbis have imagined . . . [for] they say that God has united Himself to ten very pure intelligences called *sefira* and that He operates with them in such a way that all variations and all imperfection of effects must be attributed to them. . . . We do not need to go to this extent in order to save the simplicity and the immutability of the ways of God. We need do nothing more than to establish the hypothesis of occasional causes, provided that we need explain only the phenomena relating to material bodies, and that we do not consider man. The heavens and the rest of the universe declare the glory, the power, and the unity of God. Man alone, that masterpiece of His creation among things visible, man alone, I say, furnishes very great objections against the unity of God. I will tell you why.

Man is full of contradiction.

Man is wicked and unhappy. Everyone knows this by his own experience and by the relations which he is obliged to maintain with his fellow beings. One need live no more than five or six years in order to be perfectly convinced of these two points. Those who live long and participate in the affairs of the world realize it even more clearly. Travels teach us lessons constantly on this subject. They show us everywhere the monuments of unhappiness and the wickedness of man; everywhere we find prisons and hospitals, gallows, and beggars. Here you see the ruins of a once flourishing city. Elsewhere you cannot even find the ruins of it.

> Fields of grain now grow where Troy once was,
> The ground made rich with Phrygian blood.
> (Ovid)

Read these fine words taken from a letter written to Cicero. "Returning from Asia and sailing from Aegina towards Megara, I gazed upon the countries on every side of me. Behind me was Aegina, before me Megara, on my right hand Piraeus, on my left Corinth. These cities were once in the most flourishing condition, but now they lie in ruins."

Studious men are the ones who acquire the most light on these two points, because without leaving their places of study they need do nothing more than read history in order to pass in review all ages and countries of the world. Properly speaking, history is only a record of the crimes and the misfortunes of the human race.

But let us take notice that these two evils, one moral and the other physical, are not the only subject of all history and are not the only experience of individuals. Everywhere we find both moral good and physical good, a few examples of virtue, and a few examples of happiness, and herein lies the difficulty. For if the world were made up only of the wicked and the unhappy, there would be no need of the hypothesis of two principles, because it is the mixture of happiness and virtue with misery and vice which requires this hypothesis. Here we find Zoroaster's strong point. . . .

Two principles are necessary to
explain the contradictions in man.

In order to see how difficult it would be to refute this false system, and so that we may realize that we must have recourse to the light of revelation in order to ruin it, let us imagine here a dispute between Melissus and Zoroaster, both of whom were pagans and keen philosophers. Melissus, who recognized only one principle, would first say that his system agrees admirably with the ideas of order. The necessary Being is not limited and is therefore infinite and almighty and consequently one. It would therefore be monstrous and contradictory to imagine that He had no attribute of goodness, or that He had the greatest of all vices, that is, an essential malice. "I grant you," Zoroaster would answer, "that your ideas are very coherent, and I willingly confess that in this respect your hypothesis surpasses mine. I will not insist upon an objection I might use, which would be to say that since the infinite must include all that is real, and since evil is not less a real being than good, the universe requires that there should be both wicked and good beings. Therefore, since the sovereign good and the sovereign evil cannot both exist in one subject, there must necessarily be in nature one being who is essentially good and another who is essentially evil. I do not insist, I say, on this objection. I grant you the advantage of agreeing more nearly with the ideas of order than I do.

"But explain to me, I ask you, by your hypothesis, why man is evil and so subject to grief and pain. I defy you to find the reason for this phenomenon in your hypothesis as I find it in mine. Here I regain the advantage. You surpass me in the beauty of ideas and in *a priori* reasons. I surpass you in the explanation of experience and in *a posteriori* reasons. Now since the principal characteristic of a good system is the capacity to explain the facts of experience, and since nothing more than the inability to explain them is a proof that a hypothesis is not sound, however fine it might appear in other respects, you will have to admit that I hit the mark in admitting two principles and you do not hit it by admitting only one."

Here we are at the heart of the question, and here Melissus has a splendid opportunity to rise to the occasion. But let us see what Zoroaster has yet to say.

"If man is the creation of a single principle which is sovereignly good, sovereignly holy, and sovereignly powerful, can he be exposed to sickness, cold, heat, hunger, thirst, pain, and grief? Is it possible for him to have so many wicked inclinations? Is it possible for him to commit so many crimes? Is it possible for the Sovereign Holiness to produce a criminal creature? Is it possible for the Sovereign Goodness to produce an unhappy creature? Could Omnipotence joined to infinite goodness do any other than supply His work abundantly with good things? Would He not protect it from everything which could offend it or give it pain?"

Human liberty does not explain evil.

If Melissus consults the ideas of order, he will reply that man was not wicked when God made him. He will say that man was originally endowed with a condition of happiness by God, but not having followed the light of his conscience which his Creator intended should guide him in the path of virtue, he became wicked and deserving of the anger of a sovereignly just and good God. Therefore, it is not God who is the cause of moral evil, but He is the cause of physical evil, which is the punishment of moral evil. This punishment is far from being incompatible with the sovereign goodness of the Creator because it emanates necessarily from one of His attributes, that is, His justice, which is not less essential to Him than is goodness.

This answer, the most reasonable that Melissus can make, is basically good and sound, but it can be opposed by reasons which are more specious and dazzling, for Zoroaster would not fail to point out that if man were the work of a single infinitely good and holy principle, he would have been created not only without any present evil but also without any inclination to evil, since this inclination is a defect which cannot have such a principle as its cause. All that Melissus can say, therefore, is that man as he came from the hands of his Creator had only the power of choosing evil, and having made this choice, he alone is the cause of the crime which he committed and of the moral evil which was introduced into the world.

However, we must first remember that we have no distinct idea which gives us to understand that a being who is not self-existent can act by himself. Zoroaster will then say that the free agency given to man is not capable of causing a present determination, since man exists constantly and totally by the action of God. He will next raise this question: did God foresee that man would make an unfortunate use of his free agency? If the answer is affirmative, he will reply that it does not seem possible to foresee anything the cause of which is not predetermined. "But," he will go on to say, "I will grant you that God foresaw the sin of His creature, and I conclude from that that He could have prevented him from sinning because the ideas of order do not permit us to suppose that an infinitely good and holy Being did not prevent the introduction of moral evil into the world if He were able, especially if in permitting its introduction, He saw Himself obliged to heap punishments upon his own creature. If God did not foresee the fall of man, He at least judged that it was possible. As He saw that in this eventuality He would be obliged to depart from His paternal goodness and render His children miserable by assuming to them the relation of a severe judge, He should have inclined man toward moral good as He has inclined him toward physical good. He would have left in the soul of man no power by which he could give himself over to sin, just as He has left man no power to seek misery as such. This is the conclusion that we are led to by our clear and distinct ideas of order when we follow step by step what an infinitely good principle should do. For if a goodness as limited as that of earthly fathers requires necessarily that they prevent as much as possible the ill-usage which their children could make of the goods which they give, how much more might we suppose that an infinite and omnipotent Goodness will prevent evil effects of His gifts. Instead of granting free agency, He will incline His creatures to good, and if He gives them free agency, He will keep strict watch to prevent them from sinning." Here Melissus would undoubtedly not remain silent, but everything which he could answer would be opposed immediately by reasons which are just as plausible as his, and thus the dispute would never end.

Zoroaster's supposition

Zoroaster would be hard pressed if Melissus cast back the same argument but once he were granted his two principles, he would have an open road to arrive at an explanation of the origin of evil. He would go back to the time of the chaos which, with regard to his two principles, is a period similar to the "state of nature" that Thomas Hobbes supposed to have preceded the establishment of society. In this state of nature each man was as a wolf to all other men, and everything belonged to its first possessor. No one was master of anything unless he happened to be the strongest. In order to be delivered from this confusion, each one agreed to abandon his claim upon everything so that the others would agree to let him possess something. Compromises were made, and the state of war ceased. In like manner Zoroaster might suppose that since his two principles had become weary of the chaos where each would confound and frustrate the purposes of the other, they agreed to compromise. Each one had his part in the production of man and in the laws of the union of the soul. The good principle obtained those laws which procured man his numerous pleasures and consented to those which exposed man to his numerous pains. If he consented to the proposal that moral good was to be infinitely less in the human race than moral evil, he obtained that in some other kinds of creatures there would be less vice than virtue. If a number of men in this life experience more misery than happiness, compensation is made in another state: what they do not receive as human beings they recover elsewhere. (Notice that all those, or at least most of those, who have admitted two principles, have believed in the transmigration of souls.) This compromise ended the confusion of the chaos, a passive principle which was the battlefield of the two active principles. (The poets have represented the dissipation of this confusion under the image of a quarrel ended.) That is what Zoroaster could allege, priding himself in not making the good principle the willing creator of a work which was to be so wicked and miserable as man, for Zoroaster imagines that He would consent to such a creation only after realizing that He could not more successfully oppose the horrible purposes of the wicked principle. In order to make his hypothesis less shocking, he could deny that there was a long war between these principles and could do away with all the combats and prisoners of which the Manicheans have spoken. He would need to retain nothing more than the supposition that the two principles knew they could obtain only such and such conditions. An eternal agreement could have been made on these grounds.

Reason is too weak to solve the difficulty.

A thousand formidable difficulties could be raised to Zoroaster, but since he would find possible answers and, in the end would ask you to furnish a better hypothesis (claiming to have roundly refuted the hypothesis of Melissus), he would never be brought around to the point of truth. Human reason is too weak for that. It is a principle of destruction and not of edification. It is fit only to form doubts, to turn to the right and to the left, and to draw out a dispute eternally. I do not believe I would be mistaken in speaking of the natural revelation (the light of reason) in the same way that the theologians speak of the Law of Moses, which, according to them, was fit only to make known to man his impotence and the necessity of a Redeemer and a law of mercy. In their words, it was a "schoolmaster to bring us to Jesus Christ." Let us make a similar remark concerning reason. It is fit only to make known to man his ignorance, his impotence, and the necessity of another revelation, which is that of the Scripture. It is here that we find the means of invincibly refuting the hypothesis of the two principles and the objections of Zoroaster. We find here the unity of God and his infinite perfections, the fall of the first man and everything that follows. Then if we are told with a great show of reasonings that it is not possible for moral evil to be introduced into the world by the workings of an infinitely good and holy principle, we will answer that such has nonetheless been the case and that consequently it is very possible. There is nothing more foolish than to reason against facts. The axiom *ab actu ad potentiam valet consequentia* [what has happened is possible] is as clear as the proposition that two and two are four.

The Manicheans were aware of what I have just said. For that reason they rejected the Old Testament, but the part of the Scripture which they retained furnishes sufficient arms to the orthodox. Thus it was not too difficult to confound these heretics who, moreover, entangled themselves childishly when they came to speak of particulars. [See Remark B.] Now since it is the Scripture which furnishes the best solution to the question, I was not wrong in saying that a pagan philosopher would be difficult to rout on this matter. This is the text of this remark. . . . [Bayle promises to continue the discussion in the article "Paulicians."]

Remark E. . . . *his zeal was supported by the imperial laws.* . . .

      [Bayle recounts the activities of the Manichean sect in Rome and tells of the civil measures taken against them.]

Remark F. . . . *they permitted their hearers to practice it in favor of the elect.*

      [Bayle comments on the differences between the two classes of Manicheans.]

Paulicians.   This was the name given to the Manicheans in Armenia when a certain Paul became their leader in the seventh century. "They managed to attain to such a great power, either by the weakness of the government or by the protection of the Saracens, or even by the favor of the emperor Nicephorus who was very attached to this sect, that when they were persecuted by the Empress Theodora, wife of Basil, they found themselves capable of building cities and taking arms against their princes. These wars were long and bloody under the empire of Basil the Macedonian, that is, near the end of the ninth century." [1] Nevertheless, there had been such a great slaughter among these heretics under the Empress Theodora (A), that the world believed they would never be capable of recovering from it. It is believed that the preachers which they sent into Bulgaria (B) established the Manichean heresy there, and from that place it soon spread throughout all the rest of Europe. The Paulicians condemned the worship of the saints and the images of the cross (C), but this was not their principal characteristic. Their fundamental doctrine was that of the two co-eternal principles which were independent one from another. This dogma inspires horror at first, and consequently it is strange that the Manichean sect was able to deceive so many people (D). On the other hand, it is so difficult to answer its objections concerning the origin of evil (E) that it is not astonishing that the hypothesis of the two principles, one good and the other evil, dazzled several ancient philosophers and found so many disciples in Christianity where the doctrine which teaches the enmity of the devils to the true God is always accompanied by the doctrine which teaches the rebellion and fall of one part of the good angels. This hypothesis of the two principles would apparently have made more progress if the details had been given a little less grossly and if it had not been accompanied by several odious practices [see remark B in the article on Manicheans], or if there had been at that time as many disputes concerning predestination as there are today (F), in which the Christians accuse each other either of making God the author of sin or of depriving Him of the government of the world. The pagans could answer the Manichean objections better than could the Christians (G), but several of their philosophers found themselves in much difficulty in doing so. I shall observe in what way the orthodox seem to admit two first principles (H), and in what sense we cannot say that the Manicheans make God the author of sin (I). I will also

[1] Mr. De Meaux, *History of the Variations,* Book 11, Number 13, page 128.

criticize a modern writer who denies that the doctrine
which makes God the author of sin leads to irreligion. He
has even said that this doctrine raises God to the highest
degree of grandeur which can be conceived. The ancient
fathers were not unaware that the question of the origin of
evil was very embarrassing (K). They were not able to re-
solve it by the hypothesis of the Platonists which in the final
analysis was a branch of Manicheanism (L), since it admitted two principles. They were obliged to have recourse
to the free will of men. However, the more we reflect on
that way of solving the difficulty, the more we find that the
natural light of philosophy further entangles this Gordian
knot (M). A learned man claims that the Pythagoreans gave
rise to this difficult question. In their questionings they
always sought the superlative; they would ask, for example,
what is the strongest, the oldest, the commonest or the
truest thing in the world. They were once answered with
regard to this last point that God is good and men are
wicked. This led to another question: why are men wicked
if God is good? (N) The answer to this question appeared
very important to Simplicius.

*Remark A. There had been such a great
slaughter among these heretics under the
Empress Theodora.* [Bayle here gives the
details of the persecution of the Paulicians
and observes that Christians have been
more intolerant than the Mohammedans.]

*Remark B. . . . the preachers which they
sent into Bulgaria* [Bayle traces the growth
of the Manichean heresy.]

*Remark C. The Paulicians condemned the
worship of the saints and the images of the
cross.* [Bayle gives an historical anecdote to
this effect.]

Remark D. . . . it is strange that the
Manichean sect was able to deceive so
many people. [Bayle indicates the extent
of the Manichean heresy throughout its
history.]

Remark E. It is extremely difficult to
answer the objections of the Manicheans
concerning the origin of evil.

I have prepared my readers to consider three observations which I would have put in the article on the Manicheans, if I had not wished to avoid undue length in that
place. But I will now acquit myself of my promise and will
not frustrate the expectations of those who desire to follow
my cross reference. Below I will consider separately the
second and third observations, but here is the first:

Christians must depend solely on the
authority of revelation in refuting the
objections of heretics concerning evil.

The fathers of the Church, who so roundly refuted the
Marcionites [a Manichean offshoot], the Manicheans, and
in general all those who admitted two first principles, have
not so well answered the objections which concern the
origin of evil. They should have frankly abandoned all *a*
priori reasons as being vulnerable and indefensible outposts
of a fortress. They should have depended only upon *a pos-*
teriori reasons and withdrawn all of their forces behind
this redoubt. The Old and New Testaments are two parts
of a revelation which confirm one another. Therefore, since
these heretics recognize the divinity of the New Testament,
it would not have been difficult to prove to them the
divinity of the Old, after which it would have been easy to
ruin their objections by showing them to be contradicted
by revealed fact. According to the Scripture there is only

one principle of good, and nonetheless moral and physical evil found their way into the human race. It is therefore not against the nature of the good principle both to permit the introduction of moral evil and to punish crime, for it is not more evident that four and four are eight than it is evident that an event is possible if it has happened. *Ab actu ad potentiam valet consequentia* is one of the clearest and most incontestable axioms of all metaphysics. Now here we find an invulnerable rampart, and that is sufficient to insure the victory of the orthodox even though their *a priori* reasons might be refuted. But is it true that they can be refuted? I will answer, "Yes," for the way in which evil was introduced into the world under the dominion of a Supreme Being who is infinitely good, all wise, and all powerful is not only inexplicable but even incomprehensible. Therefore, when we undertake to explain why this Being permitted evil, we are confronted on every side with objections which are more in accord with our natural light of understanding and with our ideas of order than is our explanation.

Evil was a necessary element of God's plan, according to some philosophers.

Examine closely the following passage in the writings of Lactantius. It contains an answer to an objection raised by Epicurus. " 'God,' says Epicurus, 'either desires to destroy evil and cannot, or else He can and will not; or else He neither can nor will, or else He is both able and willing. If He wishes to destroy evil and cannot, He is weak, and we cannot assign this attribute to God. If He is able and not willing, He is malevolent, another attribute which is equally foreign to God. If He is neither able nor willing, He is both weak and malevolent, in which case He cannot be God. And if he is both willing and able, which attributes we must necessarily associate with God, from whence comes evil? And why does He not destroy it?' I know that most philosophers who assert a divine providence are usually troubled by this argument and are almost led in spite of themselves to admit that God does not intervene in the affairs of the world, which is the conclusion Epicurus most desired to prove. But in thinking clearly on this subject we find reasons by which we can easily refute this formidable argument, for God can do anything He desires, and moreover, there is no weakness nor evil in Him. Consequently, He is able to destroy evil but does not desire to do so, and He is not for that reason malevolent either. Now this is why He does not destroy evil: it was God's good pleasure, as I have previously shown, that we should find more good and delight in seeking wisdom than in following after evil. Furthermore, it is by wisdom that we come to know God and thus to gain immortality, which is the highest good. Now if we did not first know evil, we would not be able to know good either, for neither Epicurus nor anyone else saw that if evil were destroyed, wisdom would be destroyed also; no trace of virtue would remain in man, because virtue is achieved only by enduring and overcoming the harshness of evil. Consequently, if we enjoyed the slight advantage of having evil suppressed, we would also be deprived of the greatest advantage and most real and substantial of goods, which is wisdom. It is therefore evident that all things visible in the world, both good and evil, exist for the benefit of man."

*The necessity of evil is contradicted
by theology and experience.*

It is impossible to state the force of the objection more honestly. Epicurus himself would not have advanced it more clearly or more vigorously. (Observe that this objection of Epicurus, which concerns only physical evil, would be still more troublesome if it also concerned moral evil.) But the answer of Lactantius is pitiful. It is not only weak but also full of errors and perhaps even of heresies, for it supposes that God could have brought us to know neither wisdom, nor virtue, nor the idea of good without Himself being first obliged to produce evil. Is there anything more monstrous than this doctrine? Does it not unhinge everything that the theologians tell us of the happiness of Paradise and the state of innocence? They tell us that in the Garden of Eden, Adam and Eve experienced without any kind of detraction all of the enjoyments which this charming and delightful place afforded them. They add that if our first parents had not sinned, both they and all of their descendants would have enjoyed this happiness without being subject either to sickness or sorrow and that the animals and the elements of nature would never have been inimical to them. It was their sin which exposed them to cold and to heat, to hunger and thirst, to pain and sorrow, and to the enmity of the animal kingdom. Far from saying, therefore, that man could not acquire virtue and wisdom without physical evil, as Lactantius assures us, we must maintain on the contrary that man was subject to this evil only because he abandoned virtue and wisdom. If the doctrine of Lactantius were sound, we would necessarily have to assume that all of the holy angels are subject to endless discomforts and that the souls of the blessed pass alternately from joy to sorrow, and if this were so, one would not be immune to adversity even in the celestial glory and in the midst of the beatific vision. Nothing is more contradictory to the unanimous findings of the theologians and of sound reason than is this idea. It is even true, according to sound philosophy, that the soul does not need to experience evil in order to taste the good and that it is unnecessary for us to pass successively from pleasure to pain and from pain to pleasure in order to discern that pain is an evil and that pleasure is a good. And thus the doctrine of Lactantius is just as shocking to the light of reason as to the light of theology. We know by experience that our soul cannot feel pleasure and pain at the same time. It must necessarily be, then, that it felt either pain before pleasure or pleasure before pain. If its first sensation was that of pleasure, it found this state agreeable even though it was unaware of pain. And if its first sensation was that of pain, it found this state disagreeable even though it was as yet unaware of pleasure. Now suppose that its first sensation lasted for several consecutive years without any interruption, and you will surely understand that during that time it found itself either in an agreeable state or a disagreeable state. Is this idea contradicted by experience? No, for if you point out that a pleasure which lasts for a long time becomes feeble or insipid, or that pain eventually becomes endurable, I will answer that it is only the faculty of perception which changes and that a continuous sensation may be of the same kind but may change in degree. . . . However, if pain or joy were communicated to us in this same degree for a hundred consecutive years we would be just as unhappy or just as happy the hundredth year as the first day. We see here a conclusive proof that a creature can be happy by a continuous good or unhappy by a continuous evil and that the solution proposed by Lactantius is therefore not propitious. It is founded neither upon the nature of good and evil, nor upon the nature of the receiving subject, nor upon the cause which produces sensation. Pleasure and pain are not less susceptible to communication the second moment than the first, and the third moment than the second, and so forth. Our soul also is as susceptible to experiencing them a second moment as to experiencing them the first, and God Who gives them is not less capable of producing them a second time than the first. That is what we learn in examining the ideas that we have of these subjects naturally. And Christian theology concurs completely in these ideas, since we learn therein that the torments of the damned will be eternal and continuous, just as keen at the end of a hundred thousand years as the first day and that on the other hand, the pleasures of Paradise will endure eternally and continuously without ever becoming dulled. If we might suppose that there were two suns in the world, one of which would rise when the other was setting, I would be curious to know whether darkness would be unknown to the human race. According to the fine philosophy of Lactantius, we would have to conclude that man would not know what light was, that he would not be aware that it was day, or that he saw objects, etc.

On rational grounds the Paulician doctrine gives a more satisfactory solution to the problem of evil than does the Christian doctrine.

What I have just said gives invincible proof, it seems to me, that one would gain no ground against our Paulicians by arguing that God has intermingled good and evil in the world only because he foresaw that unalloyed good would appear to us insipid after a short time. They would answer that this property is not contained in the idea which we have of good and that it is in direct contradiction with the usual doctrine upon the happiness of Paradise. And now suppose that we bring up our argument derived from personal experience which teaches us only too much (1) that we perceive the joys of this life only to the extent that they deliver us from some disagreeable state (2), that we become sated with them if they last more than a short time. The Paulicians would maintain that this phenomenon is inexplicable if we do not turn to their hypothesis of two opposing principles. For they will say that if we depend only upon a single first cause which is all-powerful, infinitely good, infinitely free, and which governs all beings according to the good pleasure of its will, we should not feel any evil, all of our goods must be pure, and we should not find the least distaste in them. The Author of our being, if He is infinitely beneficent, should take a continual pleasure in making us happy and of preventing everything which could trouble or diminish our joy. This is a characteristic contained essentially in the idea of the sovereign good. It is impossible that the fibers of our brain should be the cause for God diminishing our pleasures, for according to you He is the sole author of matter. He is all-powerful, and nothing prevents Him from acting according to the entire extent of His infinite goodness. He has only to will that our pleasures should not depend upon the fibers of our brain, and if He wills that they depend upon it, He may preserve these same fibers eternally in the same condition. He has only to will either that they should not deteriorate or that the deterioration that they suffer should be promptly repaired. Therefore you cannot explain your experiences except by our hypothesis of two opposing principles. If we experience pleasure, it is the good principle which gives it to us, but if we do not experience it without alloy and if we soon find it flat and vapid, it is because the principle of evil is working at cross purposes with the principle of good. The latter pays the former in the same money. He causes that the pain becomes less keen when we become used to it and that we always have some resource even in the midst of the greatest evils. That and the good use that we often make of adversity, and the evil use that we often make of good fortunes, are phenomena which are explained admirably well according to the Manichean hypothesis. These are things which lead us to suppose that the two principles have entered into an agreement by which they reciprocally limit their operations. The principle of good cannot do us all of the good which He would desire, for in order for Him to do us much good, it would have been necessary for Him to consent that His adversary should cause us just as much evil because without this mutual consent, the chaos would have remained chaos perpetually, and no creature would have ever experienced good. Thus the Supreme Good having found that it was better to see the world alternately happy and unhappy than never to see it happy at all, entered into an agreement which produced the mixture of good and evil which we see in the human race. In according omnipotence to your principle and in giving Him the honor of being the only eternal Being in the universe, you take away from Him the most important of His attributes, for when the most learned nations speak of God, they are not so much concerned with the number of His attributes as with the quality of His attributes. On the other hand, you have deprived Him of an attribute which is superior to all the rest. You suppose that having nothing to hinder Him from bestowing all good gifts upon His creatures, He nonetheless oppresses them with evils, and if He advances any of them it is only that their fall may be the greater. We exonerate Him completely in this manner. Without calling His goodness into question we explain all the problems that can arise concerning the inconstancy of fortune, the jealousy of fate, and the continual sport which, according to Aesop, is the pastime of God, that of raising things that are low and abasing things that are high. We say that He could obtain no more from His adversary. His goodness extends as far as it can. If He does us no more good, it is because He cannot. We have no reason therefore to complain.

Who will not marvel at and deplore the fate of our reason? Here the Manicheans with an altogether absurd and contradictory hypothesis explain the facts of our existence a hundred times better than do the orthodox with their hypothesis which is so just, so necessary, and so compellingly true of one infinitely good and omnipotent first principle.

Man cannot be the origin of evil.

Let us show by another example the little success of the Church Fathers in their disputes with these heretics concerning the origin of evil. Here follows a passage from St. Basil: ". . . to say that evil did not proceed from God is a pious assertion, for no contrary can arise from its own contrary . . . but if evil is not innate (as you maintain) and does not proceed from God, where does it come from? For no man will deny that evil exists. What then must be said?

My answer is that evil is not a living essence endowed with a soul, but is a quality of the soul, contrary to virtue. It is planted in the slothful and lazy because they have fallen from good. Do not therefore look about and inquire abroad for the origin of evil, nor seek to explain it by an essentially malicious first principle, but let every man acknowledge that he himself is the author of his own wickedness. It is true that those things that happen to us come sometimes from nature (such as old age and infirmity) sometimes of themselves (such as sudden accidents from external causes) . . . but partly we are within our own power. We are able to mortify our desires, to moderate our passions, to govern passions, to return injury for injury, to speak truth or untruth, to be of a meek and even temper, or to be puffed up with pride and arrogance. Do not therefore seek elsewhere for the principles of those things of which you yourself are master, but know that that which is properly called evil has its origin in your free will and choice." The German theologian who cites this passage is right in saying that this father of the Church grants the Marcionites more than he should, because he does not even wish to admit that God could be the author of physical evils such as sickness and old age, neither of a hundred other things which come upon us from without and which happen unexpectedly. Thus, in order to extricate himself from one difficulty, he falls into another by adopting errors and perhaps even heresies. But here is another weakness in his answer: he imagines that he will get out of the difficulty and will exonerate Providence if he can only show that all vices have their origin in the soul of man. How is it that he did not see that he was avoiding the issue and simply giving as a solution the very point in which was found the greatest difficulty? For Zoroaster, Plato, Plutarch, the Marcionites, the Manicheans, and all of those who admit one principle naturally good and another principle naturally evil maintain that without this supposition, it would be impossible to say how evil came into the world. You might answer that evil came into the world by man. But how can that be? They will ask, is it not your doctrine that man is the workmanship of an infinitely holy and all-powerful being? Must not the work of such a first cause be good? Can it be other than good? Is it not more impossible for darkness to emanate from light than it is for the creation of such a being to be evil? Therein is the difficulty. St. Basil could not have been unaware of it. Why then did he say so coolly that we can seek the origin of evil nowhere but within man, when we must immediately ask who put it there? You might answer that even though man was created in a state of innocence and that his Creator was indeed the embodiment of the sovereign good, it was man himself who introduced evil into his heart by making ill use of the good gifts of his Creator. But if you give this answer, you are simply begging the question. Remember, you are disputing with a Manichean who maintains that two opposing principles collaborated in the creation of man and that man received from the good principle that which is good within him and from the evil principle that which is evil, and you answer all of these objections simply by supposing that the Creator of man is one and sovereignly good. Are you not simply giving your own thesis as an answer?

Only the authority of the Scripture is capable of silencing the objections of these heretics.

It is clear that St. Basil's argumentation leaves much to be desired, but since we have to do with a question which exhausts the resources of all philosophy, he should have retreated within his strong place, which is the Scripture. He should have proved by the word of God that the Author of all things is one and infinite in goodness and in all kinds of perfections, and that man, who came from the hand of his Creator innocent and good, subsequently lost his innocence and goodness by his own fault. There we find the origin of moral and physical evil. Let Marcion and all of the Mani-

cheans reason upon the matter as much as they wish, trying to show that under an infinitely good and holy Providence this fall of innocent man should not have happened.
They will be reasoning then against a fact and will consequently appear ridiculous. (I am assuming that these people can be brought by *ad hominem* arguments to recognize
the inspiration of the Old Testament. For if we had to deal
with a Zoroaster or a Plutarch, this would be something
else.)

Again I insist that we must oppose these sectarians only
with the maxim *ab actu ad potentiam valet consequentia*
and with this little enthymeme that *something has happened, therefore it is not incompatible with the holiness and
goodness of God.* In order to show you my reasons for so
doing, I will make the observation that we cannot approach
the question from another position without incurring some
disadvantage.

Reason is incapable of
unraveling the question.

If upon strictly unscriptural and rational grounds we
undertake to ascertain the reasons for which sin entered
into the world, we will find ourselves opposed by other reasons which have a greater appearance of truth and harmony
with our ideas of order, no matter how good our own reasons might be. For example, if you say that God permitted
sin in order to manifest His wisdom, which is more resplend-
ent in the midst of the disorders which the evil of men produces every day than it would be in a state of innocence,
you will be answered that one might as well compare the
Godhead with a father who had let the legs of his children
be broken in order to display before an entire city the skill
which he has in setting bones; or with a monarch who would
allow strife and seditions to spring up throughout his kingdom in order to acquire the glory of having put an end to
them. The conduct of this father and of this monarch is so

contrary to the clear and distinct ideas which we have of goodness and wisdom, and in general, of all the duties of a father and a king, that our reason cannot understand that God should act as they do. ("But," you will say, "the ways of God are not our ways." I will say, "Go no further. Hold to this text of the Scripture (Isaiah 55:8) and make no further pretense to reasoning." Give up trying to tell us or convince us that without the fall of the first man the justice and mercy of God would have remained unknown, for we will answer you that there was nothing easier than to make known these two attributes to man. Nothing more than the idea of the sovereignly perfect Being makes known very clearly to sinful man that God possesses all of the virtues which are worthy in every way of an infinite nature. How much more then would this idea have made known to innocent man that God is infinitely just? Could it be that if man had remained innocent, God could not have punished anyone and therefore could not have exercised His justice? No, we cannot make this supposition, because if no one would have been worthy of punishment God could have exercised his attribute of justice perpetually by refraining from punishing anyone. Tell me what you think of two princes, one of which lets his subjects fall into abject wretchedness in order that he may deliver them after they have groaned in their misery for some time, and the other who preserves his subjects in a continual state of prosperity. Is not the latter better and more merciful than the first? Those who teach the Immaculate Conception of the Holy Virgin prove demonstratively that God shed forth upon her His mercy and redemptive grace more than upon other humans. But one does not have to be deeply versed in metaphysics to know, as does the veriest villager, that it is a greater goodness to prevent a man from falling into a ditch than to let him fall in it and then pull him out after an hour, and that it is better to keep a murderer from killing someone than to torture him on the rack for the murders that he has been permitted to commit. All of this warns us that we should not enter into dispute with the Manicheans without establishing first of all the dogma of "the elevation of faith and the abasement of reason."

The doctrine of free agency cannot account for the presence of evil in the world.

There are those who say that God permitted sin because He could not have prevented it without compromising the free agency of man, which was the best gift that He had given him. But they leave themselves open to many objections. The reason they give is fine enough and has a certain dazzling quality to it, and one even finds a certain grandeur in it, but even so, it can be opposed by reasons which are more within the reach of all men and founded more solidly upon common sense and our ideas of order.

Without having read the fine treatise of Seneca upon blessings, we know by the natural light of our intelligence that it is in the essence of a benefactor to refrain from giving any gift which he knows would be the ruin of the recipient. If this were not so, there would be no enemy so bitter that he would not heap gifts upon his adversary. We also know that it is the essence of a benefactor to go to any lengths to assure that his gifts will procure the happiness of the person whom he is honoring. If he could confer upon the recipient of his gifts the ability to use these gifts well and then refused to do so, we would say that he did not long retain the characteristics of a benefactor, and our opinion of him would not be any better if he could prevent his beneficiary from making ill-usage of his gifts and did not do so by curing him of all of his evil inclinations. These are ideas which are as well known to the common people as to the philosophers. I admit that one would not be obliged to prevent the ill-usage of a gift if the only way to do so were to break the arms and legs of its recipient, or to cast him into the bottom of a dungeon in irons, but in that case, it would be much better not to give the gift. However, if one could prevent an ill-usage of it by changing the disposition of the heart and in giving the recipient an inclination toward good, one should do it. Now this is what God could have done easily if He had willed it. . . .

If humans acted as God is said to have done, they would be condemned.

There is no good mother who, having given permission to her daughters to go to a ball, would not revoke this permission if she were assured that they would there succumb to gallant enticings and part company with their virginity. Moreover, any mother who knowing most assuredly that this unfortunate event would infallibly take place and who would nonetheless let her daughters go to the ball after simply exhorting them to virtue and threatening them with disgrace if they returned home deflowered, would draw upon herself at least the merited condemnation of having loved neither her daughters nor chastity. No matter how hard she tried to justify her conduct by saying that she did not wish to infringe upon the liberty of her daughters, neither to show any lack of confidence in them, people would nonetheless answer her that her great circumspection was not called for and more befitted a spiteful step-dame than a mother. They would add that it would have been better to keep her daughters under her eye than to give them such a privilege of liberty or such marks of confidence so inappropriately.

This example shows the temerity of those who tell us that God permitted sin so as not to infringe upon the free agency of the first man. It is better to believe and be silent than to advance reasons which can be refuted by the examples which I have just given. . . .

Free agency was not a good gift.

With these reasons it is easy to show that the free agency of the first man was not a good gift, since it was given to him inviolable in circumstances where he would use it for his own ruin, the ruin of the human race, the eternal damnation of the greater part of his descendants, and the introduction into the world of a dreadful deluge of moral and physical evils. We will never be able to understand how this gift could have been preserved in man because of God's goodness and because of His love of holiness. Again, those who say that there had to be free beings in order for God to be loved with a love freely chosen, feel in their conscience that this hypothesis does not satisfy the demands of reason, for when it is foreseen that these free beings will choose, not the love of good but the love of sin, it is easily seen that the intended purpose is frustrated, and thus it is not at all necessary to preserve free agency.

Remark F. . . . if there had been as many disputes then as today upon predestination.

If the Manicheans stopped at this point they would be abandoning their principal advantages, for here are still more terrible objections which they might raise to the Christian doctrine.

If God is the First Great Cause, He is responsible for everything in the universe, including evil.

In the first place, it is not understood how the first man could have received from a good principle the faculty of doing evil. This faculty is vicious. Everything which can produce evil is bad, since evil can be produced only by an evil cause. Thus, the free agency of Adam has its origin in two opposing principles. All the power he had to do good he derived from the good principle and all the power to do evil from the evil principle.

Secondly, it is impossible to understand how God only permitted sin, for a simple permission to sin added nothing to the free agency of man and did not enable one to see whether Adam would persevere in his innocence or whether he would fall from it. In addition to the ideas that we have of a created being, we can understand neither how he can be a source of action nor how he can move himself to act. Neither is it clear how he could create any modalities within himself by any power peculiar to himself when at every moment of his life he depends wholly upon another cause for his existence and his faculties. These modalities must either be identical with the substance of the soul, as is the opinion of the modern [Cartesian] philosophers, or distinct from the substance of the soul, as the Peripatetics assure us. If they are identical with it, they can only be produced by the cause which is capable of producing the very substance of the soul. Now it is evident that man is not this cause nor can he be. If they are distinct from the soul, they are entities drawn from nothing, since they are not composed of the soul neither of any pre-existent nature. Therefore, they cannot be produced except by a cause capable of creation. Now all of the sects of philosophy are agreed that man is not such a cause, neither can he be. Certain ones maintain that the impulsion to act comes to him from without and that he can nonetheless stop it and fix it upon such or such an object. This is contradictory, since it requires as much force to stop something in motion as to move something which is in a state of rest. The thing created cannot, therefore, be moved by a mere permission to act, not having within itself the cause of movement. It is consequently necessary for God to move it, and He thus does something more than simply give the permission to sin.

God's responsibility is proved by a new reason, which is that one cannot understand how contingent events can be infallibly brought to pass by a simple permission to act, in view of the great number of purely possible things. Neither can one understand how a mere permission will permit Deity to know assuredly that the creature will sin. A mere permission could not be the basis of a divine fore-knowledge. It is this reason which has caused the greater part of the theologians to suppose that God decreed that the creature should sin. According to them, this decree is the basis of foreknowledge. According to others, He decreed that the creature should be placed in circumstances in which He foresaw it would sin. Thus, some maintain that God foresaw sin because of His decree, and others that He gave the decree because He had foreseen sin. No matter which way we explain it, it obviously follows that God willed that man should sin and that He preferred sin to the perpetual continuance of innocence which it was so easy for him to procure and command. Make that agree, if you are able, with the goodness which He must have for His creatures and with the infinite love He must have for holi-ness.

Providence is not exonerated by denying Divine foreknowledge.

In addition, if you agree with those who come the closest to exonerating Providence and say that God did not foresee the fall of Adam, you gain very little. For He at least knew most certainly that the first man would run the risk of losing his innocence and introducing into the world all of the evils of pain and guilt which followed his revolt. Neither His goodness, His holiness, nor His wisdom could have permitted Him to run the risk of these events. Our reason convinces us most clearly that when a mother would let her daughters go to a ball knowing very certainly that they would run a great risk with respect to their honor, she would witness that she loved neither her daughters nor chastity. Furthermore, if we suppose that she has an infallible preservative against all temptations and does not give it to her daughters in sending them to the ball, we can be most assured that she is guilty and cares very little about the virginity of her daughters.

Let us carry this comparison a little further. Suppose that this mother herself went to the ball and happened to see through a window that one of her daughters was defending herself very feebly in some secluded corner against the pleadings of some young gallant. If she then saw that her daughter had only one step to take to acquiesce to the desires of the tempter and then did not rush to her aid to keep her from this pitfall, would we not justly say that she was acting as a cruel stepdame and that she would be capable of selling the honor of her own daughter?

The Socinian doctrine does not remove the difficulty.

Now here we see the picture of the conduct which the Socinians suppose to be that of God. They cannot say that He did not know the sin of the first man except as a possible event. He was aware of each step of the temptation and must have known just a moment before Eve succumbed that she was going to succumb. He must have known, I repeat, with the same degree of certainty that renders others inexcusable and prevents them from saying, "I had some reason to believe that that would not happen," if they do not forestall or prevent evil. When a woman is ready to yield, there are few people who are so inexperienced that they are not aware of it if they happen to see by a window how she is defending herself—they do not need to know her heart—the outward signs are sufficient. The moment of consent is preceded by certain indications which are unmistakable. How much more certainly must God, who knew all of the thoughts of Eve just as soon as they were formed (the Socinians do not deprive Him of this knowledge) have known that she was going to succumb. He therefore willed to let her sin. I repeat He willed it at the same time that He saw the certainty of the sin. The sin of Adam was even more certainly foreseen, for the example of Eve gave all the more reason to foresee the fall of her husband. If God had really desired the preservation of man and innocence and had desired to dispel all of the misfortunes which were to be the infallible consequence of sin, should He not at least have strengthened the husband after the woman had fallen? Should He not have given him another woman pure and uncorrupted instead of that one who had fallen to temptation? Let us therefore conclude that the Socinian system, even in denying the foreknowledge of God and reducing Him to servitude and to a pitiful form of government, still does not remove the great difficulty which it should remove and which forces these heretics to deny the foreknowledge of contingent events.

I refer you to a professor of theology still living [1] who has demonstrated as clearly as the day that neither the Scotists, the Molinists, the Remonstrants, the Universalists, the Pajonists, Father Malebranche, the Lutherans, nor the Socinians are capable of answering the objections of those who impute to God the introduction of sin into the world and who pretend that it is not compatible with His goodness, neither with His holiness, neither with His justice. Therefore, this professor, not finding elsewhere a position more tenable, remains in the hypothesis of St. Augustine, which is the same as that of Luther, Calvin, the Thomists, and the Jansenists. He remains there, I say, distressed by the "astonishing difficulties" which he has displayed and overwhelmed by their weight.

Since Calvin and Luther appeared, I do not think that a single year has gone by without someone accusing them of making God the author of sin. The professor of whom I am speaking admits that with regard to Luther this accusation is right. However, the present-day Lutherans claim

[1] Pierre Jurieu, *Rigid and Mitigated Methods of Explaining Grace,* 1686.

the same thing with regard to Calvin. The Roman Catholics make the same claim with regard to both of them. The
Jesuits make the same claim with regard to the Jansenists.
Those who are ever so slightly equitable and moderate in
their judgments do not declare that their adversary acts in
bad faith when he says that his doctrine does not make God
the author of sin. They readily agree that he does not teach
it formally and that he does not see everything that his doctrine signifies, but they add that nothing is gained by arguing against facts—if their opponent takes the trouble to
state exactly what God would have had to do in order to
become the author of the sin of Adam, he will find that
according to his dogma, God did everything that was necessary. You therefore do just the opposite of Epicurus, they
say, for he denied in effect that there were gods and nonetheless maintained that there were gods. You, on the other
hand, deny by your words that God is the author of sin, and
yet in the final analysis you teach it.

Let us come at long last to the text of this remark. The
disputes which have arisen in the West among Christians
since the Reformation have clearly shown that no one
knows which way to turn when he undertakes to dispel the
difficulties of explaining the origin of evil. We must therefore conclude that a Manichean would be more terrible to
encounter today than formerly, for he would refute all of
us by the arguments which we use against each other. "You
have exhausted all of the resources of your mind," he would
say to us. "You have invented your *scientia media* as a *deus
ex machina* in an attempt to bring order out of your chaos.
This invention is in vain. One cannot understand how God
could foresee the future except through His own decrees
or in the necessity of causes. To make Him the author of
sin and at the same time the epitome of goodness and holiness is not less incomprehensible according to metaphysics
than according to ethics. I refer you to the Jansenists. See
how they ruin your *scientia media* both by direct proofs
and by retorting your own arguments, for it does not keep

all of the sins and all of the misfortunes of man from being according to the free choice of God. They thus leave God exposed to the analogy of a mother who, knowing certainly that her daughter would leave her maidenhood in a given place at a given hour if she were solicited by a given man, would nonetheless arrange the interview and lead her daughter there and would leave her there upon her good faith." (This comparison has shocked several persons of the Reformed Religion, but I ask them to consider that I do so only in order to pay the Jesuits and Arminians in their own money, because they make the most horrible comparisons imaginable between the God of the Calvinists and Tiberius, Caligula, etc. It is good to show them that they can be beaten with their own arms.)

"The Socinians," [our Manichean would continue], "overwhelmed by this objection, attempt to extricate themselves from the difficulty by denying the foreknowledge of God, but they are exposed to the shame of seeing that their hypothesis degrades the power of God without exonerating Him and that it only slightly mitigates the above comparison. I refer them to the Protestants who confound and overwhelm them. As to absolute decrees, which are the certain source of foreknowledge, I ask you to take note of the way in which the Molinists and the Remonstrants oppose them. And then here in the midst of it all is a theologian as resolute as Bartolus who confesses almost with tears in his eyes that there is no one who is more distressed than he is with the difficulties surrounding these decrees, and that he remains in this position only because he finds himself even more overwhelmed by the same weighty objections when he undertakes to explain grace by a more liberal method.[1] He has explained his position with even more force elsewhere, and you cannot deny that he has incontestably refuted all of those methods."

[1] Jurieu, *Rigid and Mitigated Methods,* p. 23.

PIERRE BAYLE

The Manichean explanation of evil entails
fewer difficulties than the Christian doctrines.

"You have no remaining resource to explain evil, therefore, unless you adopt my system of two opposing principles. In this way, all of the difficulties are dissipated, and
you exonerate fully the good principle. Moreover, you will
understand that you are doing nothing more than going
from a less reasonable Manicheanism to a more reasonable
Manicheanism, for if you examine your system with care
you will see that you recognize two principles, just as much
as I do, one good, the other evil; but instead of placing
them as I do in two subjects, you combine them into the
same single substance, a thought which is monstrous and
impossible to admit. According to you, the single principle
which you admit, willed from all eternity that man should
sin and that the first sin was to be infectious. (According to
the Molinists, He decreed that He would put men into situa-
tions where He knew most certainly that they would sin,
when He could have either put them in more favorable circumstances or not put them in the unfavorable circumstances mentioned). Moreover, this sin produced continually
and unceasingly all of the imaginable crimes upon the face
of the earth. Therefore, according to you, He prepared for
the human race during this life all of the woes which we
can imagine: plagues, wars, famines, pain, sorrows, and
after this life a hell where almost all men will be eternally
tormented in such a way as will make the hair of your head
stand on end in reading a description of it. Besides, if such
a principle is perfectly good and if He has an infinite love
of holiness, must we not recognize that the same God is at
the same time perfectly good and perfectly evil and loves
vice not less than He does virtue? Now is it not more reasonable to divide these contradictory attributes and to attribute
all that is good to one principle and all that is evil to the
other principle?

"Human history will prove nothing to the disadvantage of the good principle. I do not share your opinion that the good principle subjected humankind to sin and misery simply because of His own good will and pleasure when it depended only upon Him to make men holy and happy. Myself, I suppose that He consented to these unfortunate conditions only in order to avoid a greater evil and then only with the greatest reluctance. That exonerates Him. He saw that the evil principle desired to ruin everything. The good principle opposed this design as much as He was able, and the compromise that He entered into resulted in the present state of things. He acted as a monarch who in order to avoid the destruction of all his dominions is obliged to sacrifice one part to the good of the other. This comparison is somewhat repugnant to reason and seems to be vulnerable to great objections, for it depicts a first cause and a necessary Being as being something which does not do everything He wishes and who is forced to submit to compromises because of impotence. However, it is even a greater defect to think that He resolved blithely to do evil when He could have done good." That is what this heretic might say to us.

The Christians must make reason bow to faith.

Let us now finish by the good use which I proposed in making these remarks. It is more useful than one thinks to humble the reason of man. The most extravagant heresies, such as those of the Manicheans, make mock of his enlightenment and obscure the most fundamental truths. That should teach the Socinians, who maintain that reason should be the rule of faith, (1) that they are entering upon a path of error which can only lead step by step to the denial or doubt of everything, and (2) that at the same time they will only be defeated by the most detestable of all people, the Manicheans. What then should we do? We should make our understanding bow to faith and never dispute upon certain things. In particular, we should never oppose the Manicheans except with the Scripture and by the principle of submission, as St. Augustine said: "Their savants were philosophers, or rather sophists, who professed to follow only reason without giving any deference to authority. With their reasonings and false subtleties of purely human philosophy they easily troubled those who did not have enough knowledge to answer them and who could only oppose them with the Scripture and the authority of the Church, whose duty it is to interpret the Scripture according to the true meaning. And thus they perverted many by promising their disciples to unfold the truth to them by nothing more than the natural light of good sense and reason and making pass as error everything which was above reason." And it was thus that St. Augustine, who knew the strong and the weak points of this sect, wrote against them in his excellent book *Upon the Value of Faith* which treats of the necessity of belief, principally in supernatural things which appertain to religion.

Remark G. The pagans could answer the Manichean objections better than could the Christians. [Bayle maintains that pagan theology was less vulnerable to the Manichean objections because it did not propose the doctrine of a single first cause.]

Remark H. The orthodox appear to admit two first principles.

The devil cannot be referred to as the ultimate source of evil.

It has been believed among Christians in all ages that the devil is the author of all false religion; that it is he who incites the heretics to set forth their dogmas; that he is the source of errors, superstitions, schisms, fornication, avarice, intemperance, and in a word all the crimes which are committed among men; and that he was the cause of Eve and her husband falling from the state of innocence. It follows from this belief that he is the source of all moral evil and the cause of all the misfortunes and woes of man. He is therefore the first principle of evil, but nonetheless, as he is neither eternal nor uncreated, he is not the first principle of evil in the sense of the Manichean doctrine, which gave these heretics an exceedingly good excuse to boast and to insult the orthodox. "You go further than we do in wronging the good Lord," they could say to them, "because you make Him the cause of the principle of evil. You claim that He is the one who produced it. You say that even though He could have prevented it at the very beginning, He permitted the principle of evil to obtain such a great dominion over the earth that the human race was divided into two cities, the city of God and the city of the devil (See the St. Augustine's books on *The City of God*). Moreover, the former city has always been very small and during many centuries so small that it did not have two inhabitants for every two million of the latter.

"We are not obliged to find the reason for which our evil principle is wicked. When something uncreated is this way or that, one cannot say why it is so. Its nature being what it is, we must necessarily stop at that point. But concerning the attributes of something created, we must look for the reason, which can be found only in its cause. You must then say that God is the author of the devil's malice, for God either created the devil completely evil at the outset or else placed the embryo of malice in the being which He had created. Now this thought is a thousand times more injurious to God than is the idea that He is not the only necessary and independent Being. And if you say that He is the only necessary and independent Being, you are again faced with the objections set forth above concerning the fall of the first man."

It is not necessary to insist upon this point further. We must recognize humbly that all philosophy has exhausted its possibilities and that its weakness should lead us to the light of revelation where we find the sure and firm anchor. Notice that these heretics twisted the passages of the Holy Scripture where the devil is called prince of this world (John 14:30) and God of this world (2nd Corinthians 4:4).

*Remark I. In what sense we may say that
the Manicheans do not make God the
author of sin.*

There is one point upon which the ideas of the orthodox do not vary—from time immemorial they have thought that to be a Manichean and to make God the author of sin are only two ways of expressing the same meaning. When one Christian sect accuses others of making God the author of sin, it never fails to accuse them of Manicheanism. This accusation is just in a certain sense, since it is true that the disciples of Manes recognize an eternal being as the cause of sin, but from another point of view you will find they can easily deny that they make God the author of sin. They can maintain that since only the good principle deserves to be called God, this great and good name must never be given to the evil principle. Consequently, they might assert that their hypothesis removes God further than any other from all participation in evil. All others make God an active participant in evil, as the minister whom I have cited above recognizes; for he says:

> "Providing we suppose that God made a plan of all of the happenings of eternity and that in this plan it was His good pleasure to give a place to all the evils, the disorders, and the crimes which prevail in the world, we need say no more. No one will ever be persuaded that so many crimes slipped haphazardly into the plan of Providence. And if they entered therein by decree of the deep wisdom of God, it does not matter whether this decree be called permission or de-

cree, for neither will be able to show clearly how this decree is in full accord with the hate which God elsewhere manifests for sin. No matter what we do, the libertines will accuse Christians of making God the author of sin. The natural reason of men leads them to believe that if God could have prevented the fall of the first man just as easily as He permitted it, and if He opened the gate to all the paths in which men have strayed, even though He could have so easily closed them, He can be considered as the author of an evil which He should have prevented, according to His principles and the hate which He has for evil."

This same minister subsequently supposes that an objection based on the *scientia media* is raised to him, and he answers that it

"does not decrease the difficulty at all. For I can always say that since God knowingly placed Adam in those circumstances wherein, by his free agency, he and countless millions of men would be lost, it is clear that God is the original author of all evils. If a sovereign knows with a perfect certainty that in placing an armed man in a crowd he would cause a sedition and a battle in which ten thousand men would be killed, he could in the strictest sense of justice be considered as the original author of all these homicides. He would never satisfy anyone by saying that he neither gave the order to this man to strike with his sword nor commanded him to provoke this sedition. He would protest in vain that he forbade the man to do it and did not move the man's arm to kill or form his voice to call people to combat. Someone will invariably answer, 'You knew full well that this man placed in these circumstances would cause all these misfortunes. It depended only upon you to place him in more favorable circumstances, in which he would have been the source of edifying examples.' I am sure the sovereign could say nothing favorable enough to stop the murmurs against him. And if we wish to speak sincerely, we will admit that we could answer nothing in defense of God which might impose silence upon the human mind. Finally, even the God of the Socinians can be accused of being the author of sin. In conclusion, I maintain that there is no safe middle ground between the God of St. Augustine and the God of Epicurus, who held himself aloof from everything, or the God of Aristotle, who was not concerned with anything lower than the moon. Just as soon as we recognize a general Providence, the difficulty appears, and when one believes that he has closed one door, it comes in by another." [1]

That is what is called speaking clearly. But if the God of the Manicheans, and by that I mean the good principle which they called God *par excellence,* had been discovered by this minister, he might have been obliged to express himself a little differently and to confess that their hypothesis exonerates God, for they attribute all evil to the evil principle. It will not be without profit to learn how he answers his critics, for he states: "Among all of this confusion there is found an observation on what I said in another place, that no matter which methods one follows, he will never perfectly dispel the doubts which the objections of the profane raise in his mind concerning sin and the providence of God. If these gentlemen are aware of a means of resolving these difficulties perfectly, they would oblige us very much by informing us of it."

I will be told that I am wrong in recognizing that the Manicheans exonerate God by their hypothesis, for someone will point out that if they claim that God entered into a compromise with the evil principle, as stated above,[2] He consented to the introduction of evil into the world. He agreed to suffer it, and He willed positively that all crimes and all the misfortunes of the human race be produced. The Manicheans make Him more responsible for sin than do the Socinians, who hold that He did not know whether or not the free creature would sin; therefore, if He consented to take the risk, He had much hope that the light of intelli-

---

[1] Jurieu, *Judgment Upon Rigid and Mitigated Methods,* pp. 68, 69, 72, 73.

[2] See the Article on the Manicheans, Remark D.

gence in the creature, together with His threats, would turn the creature away from doing evil.

The Manicheans could answer all
Christian objections.

I do not think that a Manichean would find much difficulty in this objection, for in the first place, he could say that God entered into this compromise only as a last resort, because otherwise He could never have done any good at all for His creatures. There is therefore a great difference between Manicheanism and Socinianism. The Socinians admit that God permitted man to fall into crime and wretchedness although He could very easily have caused that man should be neither criminal nor unhappy. But Manicheanism supposes that God consented to this fall only out of pure necessity and in order to avoid an even greater evil. In the second place, a Manichean could deny that God ever compromised with the evil principle. He could maintain that He is opposing sin continually and unceasingly with all of His strength in order to render His creation perfectly holy and perfectly happy, but that the evil principle on his side is acting with all of His might for quite the opposite end. From this continual conflict results the mixture of good and evil that we see in the world, just as the action and the reaction of cold and heat produce a middle quality. Apply here what the scholastics say about the nature of mixtures resulting from the clash of the elements.

I am fully aware that each of these explanations creates a dreadful abyss of difficulties, but here the only question is to determine whether or not this hypothesis exonerates God. Now these wretched heretics claim that any difficulty is small in comparison with that which results from making God the author of sin; and it is sure that all Christians find this idea equally abhorrent. The Jesuits maintain that it would be better to be an atheist and to recognize no God than to pay supreme homage to a Being Who commands

CARL A. RUDISILL LIBRARY
LENOIR RHYNE COLLEGE

man not to do evil, and Who nonetheless causes him to commit it, and then punishes him for it. They maintain that the God of Epicurus is more innocent, and if we may speak in this way, more God than such a God. And even when the Marcionites and the Manicheans took it into their heads to create a second God who was author of all evil, they nonetheless worshipped another who was the giver of all good gifts, whereas yours, say the Jesuits to those of the Reformed Church, is worse than men.

The Calvinists, to whom these reproaches are addressed, do not reject these consequences, but they do reject the premise. They merely maintain that it is an infamous slander to accuse them of making God the author of sin. The same Jesuits claim that the doctrine of Calvin upon predestination invariably entails consequences "which absolutely destroy any idea that one should have of God and therefore lead directly to atheism." [1] The minister who answered Mr. Maimbourg [Jurieu] proves that the latter set forth the doctrine of Calvin incorrectly. He should have stopped there, because when he adds that Mr. Maimbourg drew a false conclusion from the doctrine which he imputed to Calvin, he reasons pitifully. The reader will judge for himself.

> "Besides that, I say that his conclusion is erroneous and that there is nothing more absurd and less worthy of a theologian than the conclusion which Mr. Maimbourg attempts to draw from the doctrine of these theologians, which is that the doctrine of the Calvinists destroys absolutely any idea that we should have of God, and hence leads directly to atheism. Nothing more ill considered was ever said. Let us look at the question in the least favorable light. If this doctrine destroys any idea which we ought to have of God, it is because it pictures us a God who is cruel, unjust, punishing and chastising innocent creatures by eternal torments. And this is precisely what Mr. Maimbourg means when he says that this doctrine destroys the idea of

[1] Father Maimbourg, *History of Calvinism*, bk. I, p. 73.

God, because the idea of God implies the attributes of kindness, justice, and equity; but in all conscience can we say that the idea of a severe, tyrannical, and excessively rigorous God leads men to atheism? . . . It is a foolish thought to say that a hypothesis leads to atheism when it makes God present in all things,[1] when it makes Him the cause of all things, and the only end of all of His own actions, and when it elevates Him above the creature to the point of being able to make disposition of him according to rules which even appear unjust in the carnal sense. Far from saying that the opinion of the Calvinists leads to atheism, we should say on the contrary that it elevates the Godhead to the highest imaginable degree of grandeur. For it so abases the creature before the Creator that the Creator in this system is not bound by any kind of law with regard to the creature and can make such disposition of him as seems to Him good and can cause the creature to serve the ends of His glory by whatever means He pleases without the creature having any right to contradict Him." [2]

Making God the author of sin would mean the end of religion.

Here is the most monstrous doctrine and the most absurd paradox ever advanced in theology, and I am very much mistaken if ever any distinguished theologian has said such a thing. All others have twisted every way imaginable in order to explain in what way God influences the actions of sinners, and they retained the hypothesis of absolute predestination when they believed that it did not detract from the holiness of God, but as soon as they believed that it compromised His holiness, they abandoned it. Those who have not seen that free agency is incompatible with physical predetermination have continued to teach predetermination, but those who have believed the two to be incom-

[1] The doctrine of Spinoza which teaches that all things are God Himself is nonetheless a detestable atheism. Bayle's note.
[2] Jurieu, *Apology for the Reformers*, Pt. 1, pp. 245, 246.

patible have rejected predetermination and have admitted
only a simultaneous and indifferent concurrence. Those who
have believed that any concurrence is contrary to the liberty of the creature, have supposed that the creature was
the sole cause of its actions. Nothing moved them to make
this supposition except the thought that if Providence were
combined with our own will, everything we did, including
all of our criminal actions, would be no less an effect of God
than of ourselves. They have not been at all satisfied with
the possibility that sin is not a being and that it is only a
privation and a nonentity which has no efficient cause but
only a deficient cause. Finally, some people even have come
to the point of maintaining that God could not foresee the
free actions of the creature. What is the reason for all of
these suppositions? What has been the common denomina-
tor of so many devious proceedings? It is the desire to
exonerate God; it is the clear realization that all religion
is at stake and that as soon as anyone would dare to teach
that God is the author of sin, he would necessarily lead men
to atheism. Therefore, we see that all sects of Christianity
which are accused of this doctrine by their adversaries defend themselves against it as against a horrible blasphemy
and a monstrous impiety, and they complain of being dia-
bolically slandered. And now a minister arrives on the
scene to tell us very gravely that this is a dogma which elevates God to "the highest degree of grandeur imaginable."

He does not hesitate to give such praise to a doctrine
which depicts "a cruel and unjust God punishing and
chastising *innocent* creatures by eternal torments." He calls
upon our conscience to tell us whether the idea of a tyrannical God leads us to atheism. Now if we take things at the
worst and suppose Maimbourg to be right in maintaining
that Calvin pictured a God who "created most men in order
to damn them, not because they deserved it by their crimes
but because it was God's good pleasure, and that He foresaw their damnation only because He ordained it before
knowing of their crimes"; supposing, I say, that Maimbourg

justly accuses Calvin of saying that those who suffer these eternal torments are innocent creatures and consequently that God is the author of their sin, Mr. Jurieu still cannot bear for Maimbourg to conclude that "the doctrine of Calvin destroys the idea which we must have of God and thus leads directly to atheism." He is not satisfied with claiming that nothing was ever more ill considered than Maimbourg's conclusion—he treats it as folly and ignorance and says that it shows Maimbourg to be a poor philosopher and a wretched theologian and that there is nothing more absurd and less worthy of a theologian than such a conclusion. It is a great defect in controversy not to know when to stop. This minister had very well justified the supralapsarians [1] by showing what is wrongfully attributed to them and declaring that they disavow the conclusion imputed to them of making God the author of sin. He should have retired from the field after striking this blow and should not have been rash enough to maintain that even if they pictured God as being "cruel, unjust, punishing and chastising *innocent* creatures by eternal torment"; that is, even if they held God to be the author of sin and nonetheless the severe judge who would punish this sin eternally in a person who would not be guilty of it, they would not lead men to atheism; but on the contrary, they would elevate God to the highest degree of glory imaginable.

We should ask him why it is that all the Christian sects avoid as the most dangerous shoal of all theology the admission that God might be the author of sin. Why is it that the mere idea of such a dogma horrifies us? We must admit that some people are very fortunate. If another minister had said such things, his readers would have been scandalized, and he would have been obliged to disavow this doctrine as a great sacrilege. And I am perhaps the only one who noticed this strange doctrine.

But after all, he continues, the more you involve God in

[1] Calvinists who believe the fall and redemption to be instrumental in carrying out the decree of election. [Editor's note]

everything, the more you suppose that He exists and is mighty. It is therefore very foolish to reason that "God is the author of sin; therefore there is no God." He maintains that it is false that this reasoning leads to atheism. What a poor shift this is! Let us apply this same reasoning to poets of antiquity who attributed all sorts of sins to Jupiter and the other gods, especially that of moving men to evil, and who did not even say that the same god punished them for the sins which he led them to commit. Did they not nonetheless advance ideas capable of ruining the idea of God, of destroying religion, and of turning men to atheism? Notice that there is no difference between committing a crime oneself when one has the means to do it and committing it by the instrumentality of someone else. It is clear to any reasoning man that God is a sovereignly perfect Being. There are no perfections which are more essential to Him than goodness, holiness, and justice. As soon as you deprive Him of these perfections in order to give Him those of a lawgiver who prohibits crime and who nonetheless moves men to criminal acts and then punishes them eternally, you create a nature in which no one could have any confidence, a deceptive, malevolent, and unjust nature which is no longer an object of religion. What good would it do to invoke Him or to try to be good? Where then is the way of atheism, if not here? The fear which religion gives us should be mingled with love, hope, and a great reverence. When one fears an object only because it has the power and the will to do evil and because it exercises this power cruelly and without pity, one hates it and detests it. It is no longer something to be worshipped. Does not one expose religion to the mockery of the libertines in picturing God as a Being who makes laws against crime which He breaks Himself in order to have a pretext for punishment? It is evident that one will not deprive this nature of existence while supposing that it is the author of sin, because any cause must necessarily exist when it is acting. But it will be reduced to the universe, or to the God of the

Spinozists; to a nature which exists and acts necessarily
without knowing what it does and which is intelligent only
because the thoughts of its creature are its modifica-
tions. . . .

*Remark K. The early fathers were not
unaware that the question of the origin of
evil is very difficult.* [Bayle here sights a
passage from Origen.]

*Remark L. . . . the hypothesis of the Platonists
which was really a branch of Manicheanism.*
[Bayle here gives variations of the arguments
used above in order to show that the
Platonic doctrine would compromise the
power of God.]

*Remark M. The more we reflect . . . the
more we realize that the natural light of
philosophy only further entangles this
Gordian knot.* [Bayle re-examines the
question of the Fall and human freedom
and concludes that it would have been
possible, according to any of the Christian
theologians, for God to have created
man without any defect. He then concludes:]

Here we see the defenders routed from the last of their
strong places. Will they say as a last resort that God owes
nothing to the creature and was not obligated to provide it
with an infallible and invincible grace? But why then did
they just say that He had to have some regard for human
liberty? If He had to preserve this prerogative in man and
refrain from interfering with it, He owes something to His
own work. But leaving this *ad hominem* argument aside, can
they not be answered that if He owes nothing to His creature, He owes everything to Himself and cannot act con-

trary to His essence. Now it is in the essence of an infinite and omnipotent goodness and holiness not to permit the introduction of physical and moral evil into the world.

Yes, they will answer at last, but "will the thing created say to Him that formed it, 'why did you make me thus?'" (Romans 9:20) This is well said, and we should have stopped here. We have come back to the beginning of the lists; we should never have departed therefrom, for it is useless to undertake a dispute if after having roved about for some time, one must at last shut himself up in his own thesis. The dogma which the Manicheans attack should be considered by the orthodox as a clearly-revealed, factual truth. Since after all is said and done, we must agree that we understand neither the causes nor the reasons, it is better to admit it at the beginning and stop there. We should look upon the objections of the philosophers as only so much caviling and wrangling and oppose them only with silence and the shield of faith.

Remark N. Why are men wicked if God is good? [Bayle here gives an erudite example of pagan reasoning upon the question of evil.]